A Guide to Conservation Land in Lincoln

Second Edition

A Guide to Conservation Land in Lincoln

Second Edition

The Lincoln Land Conservation Trust

Copyright © 2005 by The Lincoln Land Conservation Trust,
Box 6022, Lincoln Center, MA 01773

Maps by Margaret P. Flint

Illustrations by Paul Brooks, Scott Hecker, Gwyn Loud, and Michael
Musto

Design by David Ford

Printed by The Maple-Vail Book Manufacturing Group

Printed in the United States of America

ISBN 0-9634675-1-4

To William Preston

(1909–1989)

who guided the Lincoln Land Conservation Trust
during its first three decades

To Paul Brooks

(1909–1998)

who, through written word and generous actions,
inspired land conservation in Lincoln and across the country

To scores of Lincoln citizens

who have in the past and continue
to contribute their vision, their financial resources,
their land and their time to preserve the natural resources
and landscape that is Lincoln, Massachusetts

Contents

Preface to First Edition (1992)

Since earliest times, the citizens of our New England towns have shown a sense of responsibility, of stewardship, for the land itself. More recently, we have come to recognize the inestimable value of open land to both the town residents themselves and to the community at large, including nearby city dwellers.

Private country estates, inaccessible to the public, cannot meet this need. Hence the founding, in recent decades, of public conservation commissions and private land trusts for public purposes.

Lincoln was one of the first towns in Massachusetts to establish both a private Lincoln Land Conservation Trust and a town Conservation Commission. Working together, they have preserved over 1700 acres. How can this common land—our fields and forest and ponds—be made accessible to those who would enjoy and be inspired by them? The answer is a system of nature trails, totaling some seventy miles, described and interpreted in this guidebook. Happy hiking!

Paul Brooks   Lincoln, Mass.

Preface to Second Edition

Bill Preston (1909–1989) served as the Chair of the Lincoln Land Conservation Trust for many years and wrote guides to some of Lincoln's public open spaces which were the forerunners for this town-wide publication. Paul Brooks (1909–1998) was the Editor-in-Chief at Houghton Mifflin Publishers for 25 years and personally edited the works of Rachel Carson and Roger Tory Peterson.

Paul and Bill, to whom this edition of *A Guide to Conservation Land in Lincoln* is dedicated, were naturalists and members of a generation of Lincoln community leaders who had worked together to create a network of open space that was not only a treasure for the residents of the town but was also enjoyed every day by many people from other communities in the increasingly crowded Boston metropolitan area.

In 1992, when Paul introduced readers to the first edition of this guide, he viewed the conservation of Lincoln's landscape as a work in progress. Between 1968 and 1987, town leaders had promulgated a series of Open Space Plans that identified a large number of parcels of land that would need to be protected from inappropriate development in order to preserve the rural character and environmental health of the town. What wasn't realized at the time was that the Boston area was on the brink of an unprecedented wave of suburban development. By 2003, The Massachusetts Audubon Society calculated that 78 acres of land in Massachusetts were being lost to development every day. Even though the population of the state was growing very slowly, an unfortunate combination of economic, cultural, tax, and legal factors combined to cause the growth of vast, sprawling suburbs while inner cities declined in population and, ironically, the types of housing built did nothing to alleviate a growing crisis of housing affordability.

Lincoln, sitting close to Boston and partially protected from urban sprawl by its open space preservation activities, provided a rare, if not unique, opportunity to escape from the land use trends in Massachusetts. The laws of supply and demand functioned all too well and the value of land in Lincoln soared. The money used to buy 200 acres at Mount Misery in 1969 would be barely enough to buy four acres today. Owners of unprotected open space in Lincoln were faced with difficult choices as developers offered unimaginable amounts of money for any piece of land in Lincoln that seemed to offer the opportunity to squeeze in a mansion or two.

The response of the community has been determined and broadly supported. Landowners have continued to offer their property to conservation organizations, often at below market prices. The citizens of the town have contributed generously to land protection programs and have voted in town meeting to spend tax dollars in defense of the character of the community. The Rural Land Foundation, Lincoln's unique not-for-profit land developer, has been able to develop more than a dozen properties in ways which have limited impact on the landscape. Although there have been some disappointments along the way, the 1,700 acres of protected open space celebrated by Paul Brooks has become 2,300 acres. Additions to this edition of the guide describe several newly protected properties that are open for public enjoyment. Although more open spaces remain vulnerable to development, it has become possible to speak of a future in which approximately half of the acreage in Lincoln will eventually be protected for public enjoyment, wildlife habitat, and water supply protection.

We can already see that the heirs to this little paradise in the midst of an urban area will face their own challenges.

The Conservation Commission has become involved in difficult and controversial issues stemming from apparent overuse of the Mount Misery property by dog walkers. The water department has been forced to close trails which were deemed to be too close to the public water supply at Flint's Pond. Horseback riders, mountain bikers, and the owners of "all terrain vehicles" have all been forced to limit their activities in order to protect the trails from erosion. These will not be the last situations in which the need for wise choices about land use will tax the intellect, imagination, and good will of the people of the town.

It will also become necessary to try to help new property owners in Lincoln to realize that the very rural character for which they were willing to pay so much will be destroyed if they insist on walling off their properties, flood lighting large areas, and spreading chemicals on their lawns, unwittingly changing a landscape of farm fields and woodlots into a manicured and artificial imitation of countryside.

Finally, the people of Lincoln will need to remain committed to economic and social diversity if the town is to retain its values. As this edition of the guide goes to press, the Rural Land Foundation is proceeding with plans to construct affordable housing on its property at the Lincoln Station Mall.

The trustees of the Lincoln Land Conservation Trust hope that this guide will help those who walk the open spaces of the town to understand them more fully, enjoy them more often, and work in the spirit of their predecessors to protect them in the future.

Acknowledgements

The second edition of *A Guide to Conservation Land in Lincoln* has been a rewarding collaborative effort by many townspeople. Special thanks go to David Ford, who led us through the printing and production process and Margaret Flint, Jr., who created all the maps. They and the other members of the Trail Guide Steering Committee, Gwyn Loud (chair), Mary Van Vleck and Paul Svetz guided the project, walked the trails, researched the facts and wrote the changes. Lynne Smith edited the manuscript and Scott Hecker contributed additional drawings. Buzz Constable's expertise about trails and acquisition history was invaluable. Dwight Gertz and Virginia Welles wrote the new preface and Sue Klem was the author of the essay on changes in flora and fauna. The Conservation Commission and members of the Conservation Department, Tom Gumbart, Angela Kearny, and Jane Layton, were resources, as were Geoff McGean and Sarah Andrysiak of the Rural Land Foundation, the Lincoln Police, and Tim Higgins, Town Administrator. The support and advice of the Land Trust trustees was essential to the project. A committee of local birders, Cathleen Calmer, Vinnie Durso, Steve Ells, Winty Harrington, Norm Levey, Gwyn Loud, and Nancy Soulette, met many times to create the updated Bird List.

The following individuals also contributed helpful advice and information: Diane Abrashkin, Ken Bassett, Walter Brain, Jennifer Burkett-Picker, Linda Coca, Frances Clark, Kent Curtis, Vicky Diadiuk, Marjorie Durand, Toby Feibelman, Jim Fleming, Christy Foote-Smith, Beth Fowler, Jenny Greeson, Dagmar Guthke, Mary Ann Hales, Molly Hawkins, Sandy Hessler, Sue Howland, Avram Kalisky, Jackie Lenth, Mary Helen Lorenz, Rob Loud, Sue

MacCallum, Kimberly Madison, Sara Mattes, Ellen and Jim Meadors, Harold McAleer, Bill Mullet, Richard Nichols, Jim Parmentier, Alice Pickman, Katharine Preston, Marj Rines, Fred Richardson, Lou Sidaris, Sara Silverstein, Rob Todd, Dilla and Fred Tingley, Mary Troy, Peter Von Mertens, Arnold Weinberg, Katy Walker, Irene Weigel, Gordon Winchell, Luba Zhaurova, and Jim Zug.

Since the second edition of the guide was built upon the foundation of the 1992 edition, it seems appropriate to recognize for their hard work and expertise those responsible for the first edition. Ann Prince Hecker, Margaret Flint, Jr, Paul Brooks, David Ford, Nadie Rice, Buzz Constable, Paul Svetz, and Gwyn Loud played major roles. Additional contributors included Quincy Adams, Elaine Anderson, Jim Arena, Abigail Avery, Tom Billings, Cathleen Calmer, Jo Anne Carr, Martha DeNormandie, Dan Ellis, Steve Ells, Mike Farny, Margaret and Warren Flint, Sr., Hector Galbraith, David Garrison, Dan Hart, Winty Harrington, Scott Hecker, Bill King, Rick Lee, Bob Lemire, Betty Levin, Marcia Litte, Betty Little, Rebecca Loud, Rob Loud, Bob Mack, Sally Mansfield, Peg Martin, Mary McClintock, Mike Murphy, Sam Mygatt, Ian Nisbet, Wayne Petersen, Tony Pickman, Matthew Poole, Paula Preston, Fred Richardson, Harris Roen, Phyllis Swift, Irving Telling, Margaret Thompson, Amy Wales, Rob Webb, David Webster, and Enid and Gordon Winchell. The Conservation Commission was supportive and helpful, as were the Selectmen. Gus Browne and Lorraine Fiore managed the distribution of the books.

In writing the original manuscript, the authors also used pamphlets, brochures, and research from the Conservation Commission, Rural Land Foundation, Massachusetts Audubon Society, Lincoln Historical Society, National Park Service, League of Women Voters, and Lincoln Land Conservation Trust. In addition, the following books were particularly valuable.

The View From Lincoln Hill, by Paul Brooks. 1976.
   Boston: Houghton Mifflin.
Creative Land Development—Bridge to the Future, by
   Robert Lemire, 1979. Boston: Houghton Mifflin.
A Rich Harvest, by John C. MacLean. 1987. Lincoln
   Historical Society.
Walden: or Life in the Woods, by Henry David
   Thoreau, 1973. Garden City: Anchor Press/
   Doubleday.

It is heartwarming to realize that such a long list of contributors to the two editions of the book reflects the widespread appreciation for the treasure which Lincoln's conservation land is to us all.

Lincoln Land Conservation Trust   2005

The Lincoln Landscape

Lincoln is a hill town, a wet town, and a forest town. From an altitude of 112 feet above sea level at Fairhaven Bay, Lincoln's land rises to as high as 380 feet at the town reservoir on Bedford Road, and similar heights at Peirce Hill to the south, Tabor Hill to the east, and Pine Hill to the west. Between the hills the land is wet: about thirty percent of Lincoln's approximately fifteen square miles of land are classified as wetland. Aerial photographs give dramatic evidence of the forested character of the town, though an extensive patchwork of stone walls throughout the woods indicates that much of the forested land was once cleared for agricultural use.

Human activity has molded the natural landscape of Lincoln more gently than in many other parts of the region, preserving the community's heritage of natural beauty. Native Americans inhabited this area for a long period, but they trod softly on the landscape. Periodic burning of woodlands to produce better blueberries and some clearing for cornfields have provided few lasting remains of their presence. Native American settlements in Lincoln were probably situated along the Sudbury River, although a prehistoric disposal site, perhaps Lincoln's first dump, has been identified just north of Minuteman National Historical Park.

Colonists arrived with more demanding uses for the land. They dammed and ditched and drained. They built roads and walls, and they deforested to create fields and supply fuel. Lincoln became one of Boston's woodlots and hayfields, and then, in the mid-1800s, vegetable gardens. Many dams and ditches were built to obtain proper water levels for raising and harvesting marsh hay and to provide

water flow for small mills. In the 1840s a shift to the cultivation of upland English hay further reduced the woodlands, until finally, it is estimated, they covered no more
than one-third of the town. Arrival of the train, better
roads and increased urbanization created city demand for
vegetables, and Lincoln's farms responded with corn and
cauliflower, beans and greens. Since the end of the last century, fossil fuels have replaced wood, and better transporta-
tion systems and refrigeration have contributed to the
decline of small New England farms. In the late 1800s
many of Lincoln's open fields began reverting to woodlands. The agricultural land which remains today is carefully nurtured by the town, its landowners, and non-profit
organizations.

Geology

Lincoln has many fine examples of glacial features such as
drumlins, eskers, outwash plains and kettleholes. Drumlins
were created as our most recent glacier, with ice about
one-half mile thick, moved southward, gouging valleys and
lopping off hilltops, and carrying with it the scrapings of
the land over which it crawled. Some of this underburden
or till, which is glacially ground-up rock ranging from clay
to house-sized boulders, was plastered on bedrock ridges
as a thin sheet, ground moraine, or as "whaleback"-like
hills or drumlins. Both Hathaway Hill at Drumlin Farm
and Peirce Hill are local examples of drumlins.

As drumlins were formed during the glacier's advance,
so eskers and kettleholes were formed in its retreat. As the
glacier melted, the streams formed channels at the base of
the glacier. Eskers—cobbly, snake-like ridges of coarse
outwash deposit—accumulated in these channels. Flint's
esker, the long narrow ridge running north and south from
the intersection of Lexington and Old Farm Roads, is an
example. At the open edge of the channel the outwash
produced sandy delta-shaped plains known as outwash

plains or kame deltas. Below these, were sand- and silt-collecting lakes and ponds, most of which have filled and are bog and marsh today. This pattern of esker, delta, bog is repeated again and again throughout Lincoln. Numerous examples appear on both sides of Lincoln Road from St. Joseph's Church to Mackintosh Lane. Stranded chunks of glacial ice broke off in a variety of sizes. Meltwater flowed around them, depositing sands and gravels. The ice eventually melted, leaving kettleholes. An excellent small example exists south of Farrar Pond. Walden Pond and Goose Pond probably represent much larger kettleholes.

Poking through the glacial deposits are ledges of bedrock. These ledges are made of igneous and metamorphic rocks that formed at least 400 million years ago far from their present positions. The ledges and the valleys between them run from southwest to northeast, parallel to fault zones which developed later in geologic time when the igneous/metamorphic terrain collided with ancestral North America. Outcroppings of bedrock are easily visible at the intersection of Tower Road and Route 117 and in the Beaver Pond parcel.

Wetlands

Lincoln is a high town lying at the headwaters of three watersheds. Two-thirds of its area lies within the Charles River basin, and one-third is divided between the Sudbury and Shawsheen Rivers, both of which feed the Merrimack River. Because of its upland character, Lincoln is an island from the standpoint of its water supply. Essentially all of Lincoln's water originates as rainfall within the town, is collected by the ponds and stream basins, and flows outward. Although the Sudbury River touches one side of Lincoln, it is a collector rather than a supplier of water.

Lincoln's major water course is Stony Brook, which originates in spring-fed Flint's Pond and carries water from about two-thirds of the town's area south to an eventual meeting with the Charles River. Hobbs Brook, in the eastern edge of town, is dammed to form the Cambridge Reservoir, a large lake with wooded islands which serves as a water supply for the City of Cambridge. The Sudbury River, bordering Lincoln on the southwest, opens into the wide natural basin of Fairhaven Bay, where the river's meander has carved a steep slope; it, like other streams flowing north from the Flint's Pond basin, eventually joins the Merrimack River as it heads toward the Atlantic coast.

Because of the glacial origins and impeded drainage of much of her surface topography, Lincoln is particularly rich in wetlands. These vary in size and ecology from isolated, seasonally flooded forest pools of a few square meters, to the impressively large swamps bordering the Sudbury River. Wetlands are valuable assets to the town, not simply for their biological importance, but because they fulfill several economic and social functions, including flood control, groundwater recharge, and pollution control.

Wetlands also confer other benefits upon the town which, although less tangible, help stamp Lincoln with its unique character. Foremost among these is the habitat they provide for a wide diversity of wildlife. Naturalists have long known that the swamps, bogs and marshes of New England support populations of animals which are found in no other habitats. Vernal pools are a case in point. These seasonal forest pools may only be a few square meters in area and dry up during the heat of the summer, but they contain amphibians and other animals found nowhere else. Almost 60 vernal pools have been found in Lincoln. Wood frogs are the most common of the typical vernal pool species found in them, although many also support spotted salamanders. The much rarer blue-spotted salamander has also been reported from a couple of these pools. Of all the amphibians, wood frogs, spring peepers and salamanders visit the pools earliest in the season; warm humid nights in March often trigger their breeding activity. Later in the spring, when the wood frogs and salamanders have left, the pools may become the homes of other species such as green, leopard and bull frogs, grey tree frogs and American toads. This succession of amphibian species is one of the most marked characteristics of the Lincoln wetlands.

Such is the Lincoln landscape, every aspect of which may be found in its various conservation lands, to which this book is a guide. These areas have been preserved through the efforts of many residents over many years, and with aid from both the state and federal governments. Properly used, they will be an asset of increasing value for generations to come.

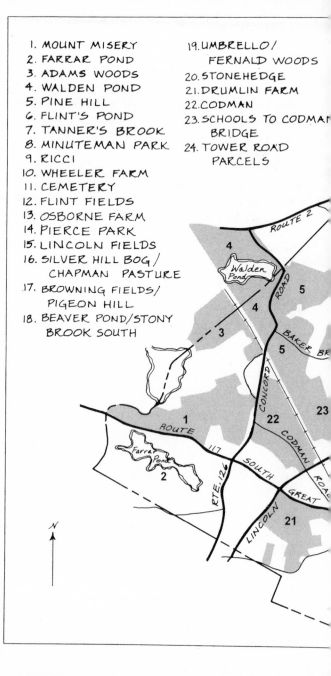

1. MOUNT MISERY
2. FARRAR POND
3. ADAMS WOODS
4. WALDEN POND
5. PINE HILL
6. FLINT'S POND
7. TANNER'S BROOK
8. MINUTEMAN PARK
9. RICCI
10. WHEELER FARM
11. CEMETERY
12. FLINT FIELDS
13. OSBORNE FARM
14. PIERCE PARK
15. LINCOLN FIELDS
16. SILVER HILL BOG/
    CHAPMAN PASTURE
17. BROWNING FIELDS/
    PIGEON HILL
18. BEAVER POND/STONY
    BROOK SOUTH

19. UMBRELLO/
    FERNALD WOODS
20. STONEHEDGE
21. DRUMLIN FARM
22. CODMAN
23. SCHOOLS TO CODMAN
    BRIDGE
24. TOWER ROAD
    PARCELS

Lincoln Conservation Land

Changing Flora and Fauna

In the fifteen years since the first edition of *A Guide to Conservation Land in Lincoln* was published, one can ponder whether the flora and the fauna in town have changed. Could there be species of plants or animals that have increased or decreased noticeably in such a short time? Anecdotal evidence from some of those in Lincoln who observe Mother Nature with a skilled eye points to a resounding yes!

Fisher and beaver have become part of the landscape. Stray moose have been reported. Wild turkeys strut across our roads. Red-bellied woodpeckers and Carolina wrens are heard regularly. In the early 1990s all of these were much less common if not rare or nonexistent in Lincoln.

Flocks of eastern bluebirds flash bright blue as they fly across fields, even during the winter. In 2005 ravens were reported in town—perhaps a first since they were driven out by the early European colonists.

The recovery and recent arrival of certain animals may be attributed to the natural succession, climate change, the curtailment of commercial trapping of fur-bearing mammals, an increase in the numbers of people providing feeders and nesting boxes for birds, and a decrease in the use of some (but not all!) toxins such as DDT. On the other hand, species are being threatened by a new wave of invasives, habitat loss due to development, chemical pollution, and new threats such as West Nile virus to birds and woolly adelgid to hemlock trees.

A surprising number of mammals began to rebound in the 1990s in Lincoln. No doubt this was partly due to attempts by the state to reintroduce some species and to the ban on body-gripping traps in 1996. Beaver were first reported on the Sudbury River. Then they moved into Farrar Pond and up tributary streams to Mt. Misery and to other areas on the west side of town. Beaver have also returned to Beaver Pond. Fisher were reported in 2000 for the first time. This has interested some wildlife experts since it used to be thought that fisher could only survive in large tracts of forested land. By the early 2000s, white-tailed deer were so numerous that people complained. Deer were being hit by cars; they were carrying the deer tick that transmits Lyme disease and voraciously eating evergreen shrubs, even those right beside homes.

One mammal whose numbers have dropped precipitously is the raccoon. Estimates suggest the raccoon population was affected significantly by rabies: 80 percent died in the mid 1990s.

As supported by the annual Christmas Bird Count and anecdotal evidence, the population of birds has changed discernibly. Not only have certain species increased markedly while others have decreased, but the total number of migratory and breeding birds in this area has declined significantly. More people feed birds by putting up outdoor feeders and planting landscaping that attracts birds. This seems to enable southern birds, such as Carolina wrens, to survive in the area. But large flocks of northern birds, such as evening grosbeaks, pine grosbeaks, and purple finches are diminishing. Still rebounding from the 1972 ban on DDT, bald eagles are reported occasionally and Cooper's hawks are often seen. After a number of attempts by the state to reintroduce the wild turkey, they are now common, sometimes observed in flocks of 20 to 40 birds. Turkey vultures, uncommon in Lincoln as recently as the 1980s, are observed regularly during warm weather, including an unconfirmed nesting pair on Old County Road one year. One theory suggests turkey vultures have moved north due to the burgeoning wild mammal population. Flocks of bluebirds have been reestablished, thanks in part to many townsfolk putting up and maintaining bluebird houses in fields. Not only is the red-bellied woodpecker increasing but also the pileated woodpecker. Record numbers of woodpeckers are drilling holes in the sides of houses, perhaps due to diminished numbers of dead trees. Mute swans, an invasive from Europe, are becoming regulars in the vicinity of Farrar Pond and the Cambridge Reservoir.

Birds whose numbers have declined in recent years include indigo buntings, barn swallows, wood ducks, eastern towhees, many species of warblers, chimney swifts, ruffed grouse, and pheasants. The Bird List at the back of this guide gives more detailed information about bird species and their abundance in Lincoln.

In spite of efforts to conserve land in town and to protect salamanders and frogs during spring migration, numbers of reptiles and amphibians seem to have decreased. Since the 1990s, on rainy nights in March that are above 40 degrees, the town has closed and monitored Lexington, Silver Hill and Conant Roads in an attempt to protect spotted salamanders and wood frogs as they travel from their wooded upland homes to temporary ponds, known as vernal pools, to lay their eggs. Observations in the late 1990s pointed to a decrease in painted and snapping turtles. Anecdotally, bull frogs seem fewer in number and, not surprisingly, their predators, water snakes.

One of the most conspicuous and unfortunate changes in Lincoln in recent times is the rapid spread of non-native, invasive plants. In spite of efforts by the town and individuals to control these alien plants, they are establishing themselves on roadsides, fields, woods, and ponds and displacing native plants. Three new species arrived in the 1990s. The black swallow-wort vine, perhaps the worst because it is dense and hard to eradicate, seems to have come into town on the train tracks. Garlic mustard, a low plant with small white flowers that smells like garlic, carpets the ground. Water chestnut grows on the water's surface among pond lilies on the Sudbury River and local ponds. Eurasian milfoil has also joined aquatic invasives. Other invasive plants, which arrived in Lincoln before the 1990s, continue to spread throughout town interfering with native plant ecology: purple loosestrife and phragmites in wet areas; oriental bittersweet, buckthorn, Japanese knotweed, burning bush (*euonymus elatus*), and Japanese honeysuckle on field edges.

As stewards of the land, both on our own property and on conservation parcels, we need to do all that we can to preserve a variety of habitats that will shelter diverse plant and animal species. For some, this will mean letting a grass field grow longer to attract grassland birds; for walkers on their favorite trails, it will mean pulling out bittersweet which is strangling trees; and for others, it will mean planting flowers and shrubs to attract butterflies. An active involvement with the land is the key to preserving our natural environment.

1

Mount Misery

General Information

The Mount Misery parcel is Lincoln's largest area of conservation land, a 227-acre property of agricultural fields, woods, hills, and ponds. The terrain varies, from the vast farm fields near Old Concord Road, to shady woods blanketed with ferns and lady's slippers, to shrubby wetlands along the Sudbury River and the new wetlands formed by beaver activity behind St. Anne's Church. Wide, well-maintained wood roads throughout Mount Misery make the area inviting to walkers, skiers, and horseback riders. The Canoe Landing on Route 117 provides access to the Sudbury River for launching small boats, where a 200-foot portage is necessary to reach the river's edge. No swimming is allowed in the Mount Misery ponds or in the Sudbury River.

Mount Misery has become a favorite destination for dog walkers from the entire Boston area. However, due to the high use of the land by people and dogs, the town has adopted regulations "intended to preserve the beauty and serenity of Mt. Misery for future generations and to make it a safe and inviting area both for people and wildlife." These regulations include cleaning up all dog feces and leashing all dogs in the agricultural fields, near the parking lots, and on a few of the main trails. Dog swimming is limited to the pond closest to the Route 117 parking lot and the Sudbury River. (See the map for details and note also the signs at the edge of the parking lot detailing where dogs must be leashed.)

Parking

Parking is available in the main parking lot on Route 117, at the Canoe Landing, 0.4 miles west of the main parking

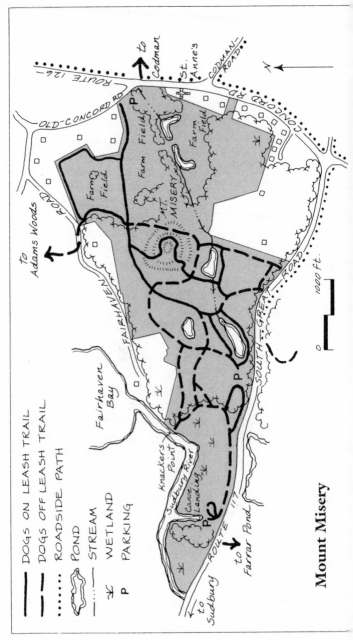

Mount Misery

DOGS ON LEASH TRAIL
DOGS OFF LEASH TRAIL
ROADSIDE PATH
POND
STREAM
WETLAND
P   PARKING

N

0   1000 Ft.

2

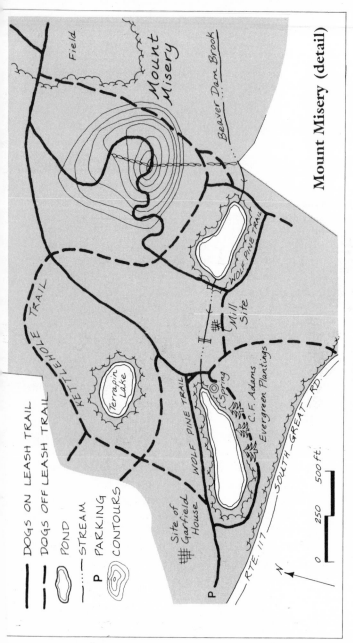

Mount Misery (detail)

DOGS ON LEASH TRAIL
DOGS OFF LEASH TRAIL
POND
STREAM
P PARKING
CONTOURS

Field

Mount Misery

Beaver Dam Brook

KETTLEHOLE TRAIL

Terrapin Lake

WOLF PINE TRAIL

Mill Site

Spring

C. F. Adams Evergreen Plantings

Site of Garfield House

WOLF PINE TRAIL

RTE. 117 — SOUTH GREAT RD.

N

0 250 500 ft.

3

lot; and in the overflow lot just west of the Canoe Landing. A limited number of parking spaces are also available at the entrance along Old Concord Road. Please obey parking signs.

Links to Other Trails

Trail links exist to Adams Woods to the north, Codman land to the east across Route 126, and to Farrar Pond to the south across Route 117.

History

Members of the Billing family were the first colonists to inhabit Mount Misery. Nathaniel Billing, Sr. obtained a deed to the land in 1667 and subsequently left it to his sons. Nathaniel Jr. and John, however, could not agree on how to partition the 114-acre parcel, especially the hill. Did they vie for the mount because it was amply suited for agricultural enterprises (aside from the ubiquitous stones)? Or were they hoping to hit pay dirt on the hill in the form of limestone and other minerals (as suggested by all the excavated areas)? Whatever the reason for the contention, the final settlement was a stone wall that bisected the summit, which still stands as a reminder of earlier times.

By the mid-1700s, Nathaniel Jr. managed to acquire a substantially larger holding, 200 acres of which he granted to his son, Daniel, along with one-half of the rights to a water-powered sawmill, midway between the upper and lower ponds where the brook comes to a natural drop. The dam built there was commonly referred to as Beaver Dam. Records show that sometime in the latter 1700s William Fillis, Nathaniel Billing's freed slave, cut 1,082 board feet of lumber that was used to build part of the Codman House (or one of the barns of the Codman Estate).

In 1788, Timothy Billing sold two and one quarter acres of his land to Thaddeus Garfield, who increased his holdings over the next 31 years. Just north of the parking lot

are the remains of the old Garfield home. Ditches located behind the foundation were probably boundary markers.

Mount Misery, according to local lore, may be named for two ill-fated oxen owned by Garfield. One day when the oxen were yoked together, they strolled off unattended and wrapped themselves on either side of a tree. Too foolish to back up, they died before anyone found them.

Through the early 1900s, the owners of Bunker's Farm east of Mount Misery cultivated a cash crop of black cher-

Blackpoll Warbler

ries and grew hay for a small herd of Guernsey cows. The Bunker farmhouse is now the red parish house for St. Anne's Church.

During the 1940s, Robert L. DeNormandie and his son James purchased the central portion of Mount Misery, known at the time as Bowen's Woods, including the old Garfield and Snelling farms. They wished to preserve the integrity of the area and prevent it from being purchased by a developer. As stewards of the property, the DeNormandies improved the wood roads for fire protection, dredged all of the ponds except the kettlehole, and built a small cabin on top of Mount Misery. The cabin was subsequently destroyed by fire.

On Fairhaven Bay, ice cutting was a big event for the Adamses and other neighbors up until the early 1940s. The ice cutting was discontinued when increased production of factories upstream began to affect the taste of the ice.

Acquisition

The 227 acres of Mount Misery were purchased by the town of Lincoln as part of a larger 570-acre parcel in March of 1969. It was the largest single purchase by the town of Lincoln, and a milestone for local conservation. After a Conservation Commission meeting in the fall of 1968, one member mentioned that the state's Department of Natural Resources was about to lose $1 million in federal funds for lack of a project to support. The meeting was quickly re-convened, and plans were launched that resulted in the

purchase of Mt. Misery, the Codman property, the Van Leer property, and other nearby parcels targeted as areas of conservation interest.

The purchase came to approximately $1.8 million. Of this, one-half was reimbursed by the federal government through the Bureau of Outdoor Recreation's Land and Water Conservation Fund, and one quarter was reimbursed through the Massachusetts State Self-Help Fund. Preservation of this area created an ecological corridor linking 300 acres of the Walden Pond Reservation, 300 acres of Massachusetts Audubon Society land, 87 acres of what would be preserved later as Adams Woods, and 5,800 acres of Great Meadows National Wildlife Refuge.

The purchase was timely. Just after the acquisition, the Massachusetts Department of Public Works presented plans to run an eight-lane highway along Walden Pond and through the heart of the Mount Misery acquisition. It is believed that the plan was set aside when officials learned the land had been acquired for conservation purposes.

Natural History

From the top of Mount Misery east to the fields by St. Anne's Church, to the wetlands along the Sudbury River in the west, the terrain is varied. The last glaciation 10,000 years ago sculpted the area, scraping the Mount Misery hillside smooth as it flowed from the northwest, plucking off the rock on the south side and leaving a steep facade on the southeast side. Below, slow-melting ice blocks left holes in the earth called kettleholes, and the movement of water under the ice created ridges of sand and gravel known as eskers.

Much more recently, humans have also shaped the Mount Misery land, as they cleared pastures for cattle and sheep, built ponds, and planted corn, fruit trees, and groves of conifers. Beavers have dammed the stream behind St. Anne's, flooding trails as well as field edges and creating wetland habitat. And time has played its part: as Henry Thoreau observed in 1860, where there once was meadow on the south side of Mount Misery, now there is forest. He wrote:

"Edward Hoar's pitch pine and white pine lot on the south side of this hill is evidently new wood. You see the green moss, the caledonia and birches (which I think do not spring up within an old wood), and even feel with your feet an old cow path and see an old apple tree enclosed in the wood. Are not birches interspersed with pines a sign of new wood?"

However they were formed, the fields, water, and woods of Mount Misery provide habitat for an array of animal,

plant and mushroom species. In August, seed-eating
sparrows and finches perch on grass and thistles in St.
Anne's fields to feed while monarch butterflies sip nectar
and lay eggs on milkweed. By the field edge, a disordered
berry-covered hedge of buckthorn, arrowwood (a vibur-
nam), honeysuckle, and wild grape attract numerous birds,
including sparrows, catbirds, and cardinals. As fall approaches, they are joined by migrating white-throated
sparrows and cedar waxwings. In summer, the symmetrical
irrigation ponds near Route 126 that separate the meadow
from cropland are colorful with pond life: yellow pond lilies, green frogs, sunfish, painted turtles, and bluet damselflies. The vast farm field beyond is also multihued: there
are verdant rows under cultivation, cornstalks, amber-
colored dragonflies, black-eyed Susans, and sometimes an
indigo bunting singing from a tree at the field's edge.
Other possible sightings are killdeer walking on the
plowed ground, a wild turkey along the edges of the field,
and a black swallowtail butterfly sailing at the forest edge.

As you step into the woods after crossing the agricultural
fields on a sunny day, the sudden deep shade may be your
first impression. The heavy canopy of conifer boughs and
broad leaves supports nesting barred owls and hawks,
which hunt for voles and white-footed mice in the adjacent
fields. Songbirds abound in the spring and summer, grac-
ing the woods with their songs: pine and yellow-rumped
warblers trill from the treetops, and wood peewees, great
crested flycatchers, and titmice are all heard occasionally.
In late summer and fall many beautiful mushrooms spring
up in the woods, including colorful species of *Amanita*,
Lactarius (the milk fungi), *Russula*, and *Clavulina* (the
coral fungi) as well as *Boletes* and their relatives. These
fungi have a vital symbiotic (mycorrhizal) relationship with
the trees. Through their networks of filaments in the soil
which are attached to and extend the root systems of the
trees, these mushrooms help supply nutrients and water to

the trees and receive necessary sustenance in return from the trees. In all seasons of the year bracket mushrooms are visible growing on or at the base of trees and on dead wood. The bracket fungi and all the mushrooms help to recycle the nutrients in the wood and replenish the soil, and are essential to the health of the forests.

A recent natural occurrence also helped to shape these woods and the surrounding area. In one day, the southeast winds of the 1938 hurricane blew down many trees, especially pines, although those in hollows or on the northwest side of Mount Misery remain standing. Today the larger trees that withstood the mighty winds of 1938 include hemlocks, black birches, ash trees, and oaks. Many of the maples and pines are young trees, but some wolf pines, much older than the other trees, also dot the woods, their giant branches spreading low from their trunks. These centenarians once had their day in the sun, marking field boundaries, with little competition for light from other trees.

Along the Sudbury River to the west, shrub swamps cover the westernmost portion of the Mount Misery parcel. In late summer, the wetland area glows with the brilliant magenta of the beautiful, but dangerously invasive, purple loosestrife. Intermixed with this flowering exotic is a mosaic of other native plants: black willow, patches of phragmites and cattails. Along the soggy river edge are various moisture-loving trees and shrubs: the speckled alder with its spotted stems and miniature cones; red maple, clothed in bright red in fall; buttonbush with little round balls of tiny white flowers; and witch-hazel, the last tree to flower in autumn, shines with yellow flowers in November.

Many of the local fauna are rather elusive. The minks, muskrats, raccoons, deer, foxes, and coyotes may leave tracks in the mud to give proof of their presence. In the spring, common yellowthroats, yellow warblers, swamp sparrows, and red-winged blackbirds feed and nest in the tangled shrubs along the water, proclaiming their territories and advertising for mates, each in its own unique way.

On the river, visible from the Canoe Landing and Knackers Point, many species of ducks and geese stop to feed and rest; and some follow the river valley as a convenient flyway north in the spring and south in the fall. Along with mallards and black ducks, you may see an occasional wood duck or hooded merganser swimming in the river, or skulking along the edge. They often visit Fairhaven Bay's shallow depths when ice is breaking up in the spring. In recent years the invasive water chestnut plant has spread in Fairhaven Bay. The Lincoln Conservation Commission has rented a water chestnut harvester annually from the State Fish and Wildlife Department to help attack this problem.

Suggested Walk: From the main parking lot to Mount Misery via the Wolf Pine Trail and back on the Kettlehole Trail to the parking lot.

Park at the main parking lot on Route 117 and head northeast on the main trail to the first intersection where a patch of red-stemmed, smooth sumac grows on the right, by the first pond. The water in the ponds resembles tea because tannin leaching out of the oaks upstream has colored the ponds the color of dark, clear tea.

Continue northeast on the Wolf Pine Trail with the pond on your right to the small clearing beside the pond. Here you can look across the pond at the Scotch pines, European larches, and white pines, the largest of which were planted by Charles Francis Adams, who bought the farmland from Stephen Garfield in 1894. The soil was depleted after many years of intensive farming and was thus better suited to support trees. Fortunately, the 1938 hurricane passed over the valley and left this beautiful grove with minimal damage. From this point you may also see some particularly lovely birds that like the pond habitat. A kingfisher is likely to fly by, chattering as it goes. These

birds perch on overhanging branches, then dive abruptly after tiny minnows. Barn swallows skim over the surface for insects, and if the area is quiet, you may see a green heron sitting very still, peering into the water for prey.

Continue along the Wolf Pine Trail following the pond edge, then turn right at an oblique angle and cut through the hemlock grove to the small bridge that crosses the stream at the upper end of the pond. Jewelweed, one of the main plants along the stream edge, grows abundantly here. Look for its light orange flowers in summertime, along with various ferns, while being aware of the abundant poison ivy, found wherever the land has been disturbed. Beside the bridge, on the far side close to the water, there is an old spring, indicated by the stones that were placed around it.

Cross the stream and follow it to the upper pond. Halfway up the stream, you may see the remains of the dam from the old saw mill site among the forest shrubs, though this is most easily seen after the leaves drop in the fall. Continue on the Wolf Pine Trail with the pond on your left to the head of the upper pond, and cross the bridge there. In May and June, the sweet-smelling, white flowers of the swamp azalea are in bloom along the south bank, and other planted rhododendrons blossom brightly, especially the brilliant orange flame azalea. The limestone fault that runs through this pond is part of a larger fault that runs northwest through Lincoln.

Follow the path up the hill and turn right at the next junction, where you'll circle round part of Mount Misery which is on your left, with a marsh and then the agricultural fields on the right. At the edge of the fields, go left onto the Kettlehole Trail, and take the next trail on the left up Mount Misery. This path takes you to the top of the hill, through a mature stand of mixed hardwoods, an occasional White Pine, and stately hemlocks.

On the hillside, it is sometimes possible to hear the flute-like song of a hermit thrush, or the crescendo call *Teacher! Teacher! Teacher!* of the secretive ovenbird, or the lively titmouse with its varied songs. Depending on the season, you may find numerous forest herbs here such as the five-pointed starflower in May, the ladder-like Solomon's seal in June, and the downy rattlesnake plantain in late summer. In winter, the evergreen ground covers such as princess pine, checkerberry, and partridgeberry with its red fruits, help to brighten the landscape.

From the summit of Mount Misery, Mount Monadnock in New Hampshire used to be visible on a clear day, and when James DeNormandie built his dandy "get-away cabin" in the 1950s, all of Fairhaven Bay and Mount Wachusett were also visible. But the views are now obscured by an assortment of large trees on the hilltop, including sassafras, some white birch, hemlocks, oaks, and hickory, and the stone foundation is all that remains of DeNormandie's cabin.

Only if you are traveling by foot (no bicycles, please), follow the trail leading down the fragile and steep southwestern side of Mount Misery. Beside the trail, in the dense shade where no green plants will grow, patches of white Indian pipes draw nutrients from decaying vegetation. At the bottom of the hill at the junction of trails, turn right on the Kettlehole Trail and follow it to its junction with the Wolf Pine Trail, where you can choose which trail to follow.

The Kettlehole Trail leads toward the river, passing through the woods and by a kettlehole, which is called Terrapin Lake because of the large number of turtles there. The standing water of this kettlehole was used to cultivate cranberries until the early 1900s, its bog-like habitat being well-suited for this purpose. You can still see the ditch that once drained water from the kettlehole to the Sudbury River on the western side of the depression.

The Wolf Pine trail to the left leads back to the parking lot where you started.

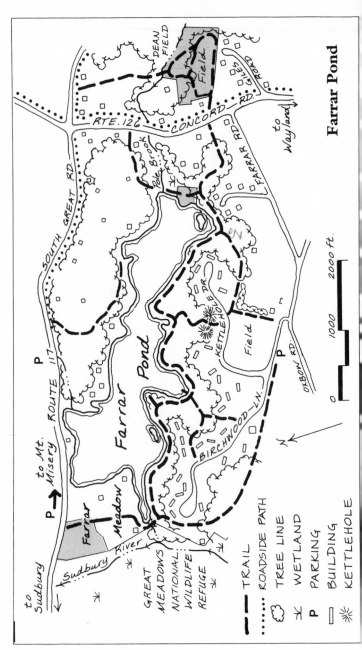

Farrar Pond

DEAN FIELD

Field

GILES ROAD

CONCORD RD.

RTE. 126

to Wayland

FARRAR RD.

SOUTH GREAT RD.

Dole Brook

POND

KETTLEHOLE DR.

Field

OXBOW RD.

P

Farrar Pond

to Mt. Misery

ROUTE 117

P

BIRCHWOOD LN.

Meadow

Farrar Meadow

to Sudbury

Sudbury River

GREAT MEADOWS NATIONAL WILDLIFE REFUGE

P

N

0   1000   2000 ft.

TRAIL

ROADSIDE PATH

TREE LINE

WETLAND

P   PARKING

BUILDING

KETTLEHOLE

Farrar Pond

General Information

Farrar Pond is located in the southwestern corner of Lincoln, just east of the Sudbury River and south of Route 117. A wooded trail winds along the west, north, south, and a portion of the east shorelines, from which a hiker can observe the beauty of the 88-acre pond and its wildlife. It is now possible to walk entirely around the pond by using the sidewalks along routes 126 and 117. Swimming and fishing are not allowed, as the pond is privately owned.

The adjoining 14-acre Dean Land, across Route 126, including fields cultivated by Codman Community Farms, has a short loop trail that encircles the area and is described at the end of this chapter.

Parking/Access

Two parking areas provide access to Farrar Pond, one off Route 117 and the other off Kettlehole Drive, both with paths leading to the dam at the western end of the pond.

The first parking lot is at the Canoe Landing on Route 117. To begin here, walk about fifty feet west along Route 117 and turn south (left) towards the pond at the driveway entrance to 17 South Great Road (Route 117). Follow this drive to the sheep fence, then continue straight ahead, keeping the fence to your immediate left and the large natural-wood house on your right. At the end of the fence, the path bends to the right and the pond in a westerly direction. The path goes over the earthen dam to the spillway, where water exits the pond and enters the Sudbury River.

The second parking lot is on Kettlehole Drive, reached via Farrar Road. Turn right on Kettlehole Drive, and park

immediately on your left in the small lot for 2–3 cars. A
trail marker among the pines, about ten feet away from the
cars and the field, indicates the trail head. A third trail starts
from Route 126 approximately a half-mile south of Route
117 where it connects to the Dean Land, but no parking is
available there.

History

Oaky Bottom, a section of lowland that would later be
flooded to create Farrar Pond, was originally part of a 666-
acre grant to colonists Thomas Stow and Henry Woodis.
In the seventeenth century, Daniel Dean and Thomas
Goble purchased the property, and, in 1684, the land was
divided. George Farrar, who was apprenticed to Daniel
Dean after his father was killed, bought the land from the
Goble heirs. He married Mary Howe, whose father gave
him his Concord holdings, so he eventually acquired 1,000
acres in the area, which extended into Concord and Wayland and included Oaky Bottom. Three of George Farrar's
four sons divided the land, and it remained in the family
into the twentieth century. According to Deacon James
Farrar, the lowland that would become Farrar Pond was
called Oaky Bottom at least as early as the eighteenth century. When James' grandfather, Samuel, marched off to the
Battles of Lexington and Concord on April 19, 1775, his
family and surrounding neighbors feared the British would
come and burn down their homes so they sought refuge
behind the Farrar house in Oaky Bottom. At that time,
and until the flooding, Oaky Bottom was a hay meadow
with a stream flowing through it. The stream had various
names at different times. In the seventeenth and eighteenth centuries, it was called Halfway Brook because it
was halfway between Concord and Sudbury (in the seventeenth century, the center of Sudbury was at the cemetery
on Route 62 in Wayland). Later it was called Pole Brook

because wagons could not enter the swamp when hay was harvested so the hay was drawn on poles behind horses.

In 1900, Edward R. Farrar decided to flood Oaky Bottom to make a pond. Some of the land to be flooded was no longer in the family, so he acquired rights of flowage from abutters. He then built a dam in the brook at a narrow channel near the Sudbury River called the gut on the western edge of the meadow, resulting in a long, shallow pond. Oaky Bottom was no more.

Acquisition

In the early 1970s, the Winchell family and the Lincoln Planning Board used innovative zoning to preserve the shoreline of Farrar Pond and sections of its upper wooded slopes. The Winchell family, who owned the property, felt strongly that the Farrar Pond shoreline should be left undisturbed but recognized that the full market value of the property would not be realized if substantial sections were left untouched.

This led to creation of the Open Space Residential District, which was formulated and approved by town meeting in 1972. Applied to Farrar Pond, this facilitated preservation of a natural landscape along the pond, managed by the Farrar Pond Associates with the assistance of the Lincoln Land Conservation Trust, and allowed for a denser development than the usual two-acre requirement on the upland sections above the pond. The first development, Farrar Pond Village, was followed in 1979 by the Lincoln Ridge Condominiums, which similarly preserved both the pond shoreline and much of the woodland adjacent to the eastern shore of the Sudbury River.

Natural History and Suggested Walk

From the banks of Farrar Pond by Route 117, there is a lovely panorama. A rippling stream called Beaver Brook runs under the road (the outlet from the Mount Misery ponds), wildflowers grow in profusion, and glossy buckthorn, viburnum, and lowbush blueberry ring the pond shore. However, if you want to see more of the pond, you must follow one of the two trails mentioned above that take you to the dam at the western end.

If you choose the path from the canoe landing, you may notice several double, white rose-of-Sharon bushes, plus a hedge of roses and the ever-present invasive bittersweet, bordering the path as it approaches the pond. In the field, listen for the songs of crickets and grasshoppers, and the twittering of chimney swifts and tree swallows overhead. The path enters a jungle of bittersweet, and just after the turn, on the right, stands a massive catalpa, which is full of white, orchid-like flowers in midsummer.

As you step onto the earthen dam just north of the spillway, you will be treated to a nearly full view of the pond. The water is bounded by large ashes, oaks, and willows on the north shore and more hardwoods framing a lone white pine on the south shore. In the opposite direction, west of

the dam's spillway, is a section of the Great Meadows National Wildlife Refuge and the Sudbury River. In fall, until the pond freezes, it is possible to see a great blue heron hunting for small bass and pickerel in the shallows. Flocks of Canada geese are commonly seen here in the evenings in the spring and fall. You may also see mallards, black ducks, wood ducks, green-winged teal, common and hooded mergansers, pied-billed grebes, belted kingfishers, several kinds of woodpeckers (downies, red-bellied, flickers and pileateds), and, in the spring, a good variety of warblers. Recently cormorants have frequented the pond, and are most obvious when they perch on a log and spread their wings out to dry. Since about 2000, a pair of nesting mute swans (an invasive species) has raised one to three cygnets here. Ospreys are regular visitors and perch along the pond or the river as they hunt for fish.

You may also see, if you are quiet, an otter, muskrat, or even a beaver swimming on the surface. The beaver returned to the pond in recent years and are making their presence more obvious as time goes on. Their lodge, with its underwater entrances, is made more of mud than sticks, and is visible on the south shore, just east of the dam. You cannot help but notice the wire cage in the water about twenty feet from the spillway, and the two tubes that extend from the pond over the spillway. Both of these contrivances were installed to prevent the beaver from building their own dam on top of the spillway; except in times of very high water, water now flows through the large plastic tubes (whose pond ends are protected by the cage), over the spillway to the stream below.

At the southwest end of the dam is a circular metal grid, which covers the equipment to control the level of the pond. In winter, the pond is lowered several feet in order to freeze (and kill) the roots of many of the pond lilies and other aquatic plants, which if left unchecked, proliferate and can quickly cover most of the pond. This is a cost-effective and non-chemical choice for weed control, installed in 1993.

South of the dam the path divides: the rightmost, narrow path is closed to the public; the center path heads up the hill through hardwood forest adjacent to the National Wildlife Refuge, to the parking lot on Kettlehole Drive via the Lincoln Ridge Condominiums; the leftmost path curves around the pond to the left, hugging the shoreline, and is described below.

The trail around the pond has been carved into the steep bank above the pond. Along this steep, north-facing grade, the trail has a North Woods aura, with hemlocks, birches, and other hardwoods, including the doomed chestnut saplings, overshadowing many species of wildflowers. Depending on the season, you will find Canada mayflower, pink lady's slipper, winterberry, maple-leaf viburnum, partridgeberry, Indian pipe and patches of hay-scented fern. The ferns and skunk cabbage unfurl early. In July the sweet aroma of the swamp honeysuckle and azalea is delicious. Likewise delicious to taste are the high and lowbush blueberries all along the pond edge. In the late summer and fall, many types of mushrooms and fungi such as oyster mushrooms, fairy ring, boletus, pear-shaped puffball and turkey feather are often seen along the ground. They can be so numerous and bright by September that they seem to decorate the woodland in purple, yellow, orange, and red. After following the perimeter of the pond for a while, you may notice that the entire water body is shallow, much of it covered with lily pads, making it perfect habitat for turtles, frogs and many insects such as dragonflies and damselflies, and several species of dabbling ducks. In springtime, frogs and numerous small invertebrates, some of them rare species, congregate in the shallows to breed.

Halfway down the pond, after you pass the dock and large collection of canoes in the cove, continue along the shore out of the cove, past the next point, to a trail junction. A turn to the right, if you are willing to climb a bit, leads you past two deep kettleholes on the steep trail up the hill through the woods to Farrar Pond Village. This trail crosses the end of Kettlehole Drive, continues along the eastern edge of the large hay field, and emerges close to the parking area on Kettlehole Drive.

To return to the parking lot by the Canoe Landing, or to explore the Dean Land, instead of taking the steep trail described above, continue due east and follow the trail as it swings north around the pond. To go to the Dean Land, at the narrow end of the pond, take the trail leading uphill and follow the directions below. To continue to Route 117 and the Canoe Landing, go towards the little boat house and dock. Continue on the path past the boathouse, over a stream, past a wet area next to the private vegetable garden, and through a field to the gravel drive beyond. You will pass through openings in two fences where you can appreciate the carefully constructed gateways, allowing access to pedestrians while avoiding the opening and closing of gates, thanks to the foresight and generosity of the Winchell Family. This part of the trail is often wet during high water times due to beaver activity. Once on the drive, turn right, and you will soon reach Route 126. Proceed left on the roadside path on the opposite side of Route 126, and go to the traffic light at Route 117 about 200 yards away. At the light turn left again, and follow the Route 117 roadside path westward. Where the side walk ends, there is a crosswalk and stairway down to the first pond in the

Mount Misery area, which will take you away from the road and back to your car. Also, just before this path ends at the crosswalk to Mount Misery, there is a trail leading off to the left. This trail was designed and created in 2004 by the Lincoln Land Conservation Trust trustees thanks to the generosity of the Massachusetts Audubon Society, which granted a trail license to celebrate their first fifty years in Lincoln. As of this writing, the trail climbs the hill, then arcs to the left, crosses a rough driveway and descends to the shore of the pond. The trail then turns left along the pond, to a dead end from which one must turn around and walk back to the beginning. While there are hopes that this trail may yet link around the pond, for now one must enjoy the different perspectives of walking first east, then west.

The Dean Field and Forests

If you wish to explore the Dean Field and forests across Route 126, when you come to the bend in the path at the end of the short eastern section of the pond, below the large stone and glass house, continue straight up the hill following the circular red trail markers. This trail winds around this new house and several others before it turns left at the top of the hill, going directly to Route 126, by the doctors' offices on the left. Emerging on Concord Road (Route 126), you may cross the road here and continue on the small path close to the house on your left. At the edge of the field, turn left and follow the edge of the field, turning right at the corner. A short way down the field, a trail leads left into the woods, where there is a marker. Continue on this trail around in a clockwise direction, taking the right turns at each of the next two junctions. (Left turns lead you eventually to Route 117.) This is good territory for finding ferns and butterflies. Several lacy marsh ferns grow in the wet sections, as well as cinnamon, royal, and interrupted fern. Abundant butterflies of the

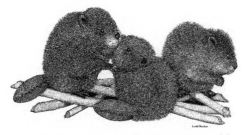

property include wood nymphs, European cabbages, sulphurs, and striking types of copper and swallowtail butterflies. The yellow- and black-patterned tiger swallowtail is a large, strong butterfly that seems to sail as it looks for nectar-producing plants, and the American copper, numerous in the Northeast, is a distinct metallic orange with little black spots. It may also be prudent to carry a compass here, as the trails are complex. It would also be wise to carry insect repellant in the spring and summer. In the spring, birds are plentiful and wild turkeys with their broods have been spotted annually in recent years. This is a relatively small piece of land and you will quickly find yourself back at the edge of the field, adjacent to Giles Road (Beware the poison ivy in the unmowed section) from which you should continue along the field edge back towards Route 126 and Farrar Pond.

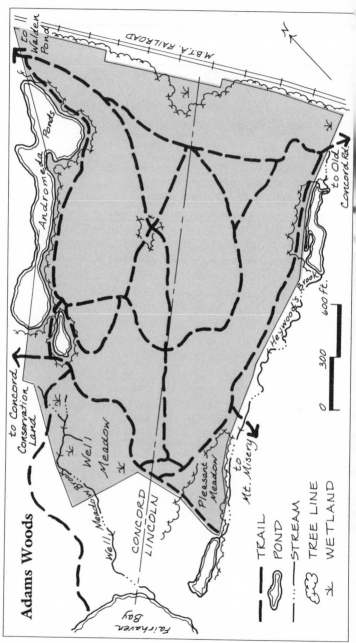

Adams Woods

to Walden Pond

MBTA RAILROAD

to Old Concord Rd.

to Concord Conservation Land

Andromeda Ponds

Well Meadow

Well Meadow Brook

CONCORD
LINCOLN

Fairhaven Bay

Pleasant Meadow

Heywood's Brook

to Mt. Misery

0   300   600 ft.

- TRAIL
- POND
- STREAM
- TREE LINE
- WETLAND

24

3
Adams Woods

General Information

Adams Woods is a 104-acre parcel which straddles the border of both Concord and Lincoln. It is under Lincoln jurisdiction. The trails meander over interesting glacial topography, a sandy kame delta with a flat top and sloping edges, and pass by numerous natural features, the most notable of which are the shallow Andromeda Ponds, a string of kettlehole bogs beautifully described by Thoreau.

The property is bordered by the Boston & Maine Railroad and Walden Pond to the northeast, Concord conservation land to the northwest, Fairhaven Bay to the southwest and Old Concord Road to the southeast. Forest, wetlands, ponds, bogs, pastures, and meadows can all be found in this highly variable terrain. The multiple habitats provide a significant benefit to wildlife.

Parking

Parking is available at Walden Pond State Reservation on Route 126 for a fee and at the parking lot on Route 117 for Mount Misery. There is also limited parking, for one or two cars, at the trail entrance on Old Concord Road in Lincoln and at the Concord Land Conservation Trust entrance off Fairhaven Road in Concord.

Links to Other Trails

The network of trails through Adams Woods land connects with Mount Misery, Walden Pond State Reservation, Pine Hill, and Baker Bridge Fields. Two important links to this extensive trail system pass over private land near Old Concord Road. We are grateful to have these critical trail easements and ask users to take special care in limiting noise, litter, and intrusions on private property when using these passages.

History

The kettlehole bogs along the northwestern boundary of Adams Woods were named the Andromeda Ponds by Henry David Thoreau. In his *Journal* on January 2, 1855, he wrote, "These Andromeda Ponds are very attractive spots to me. They are filled with a dense bed of the small andromeda, a dull red mass as commonly seen, two feet or more high, as thick as a moss bed, springing out of a still denser bed of sphagnum beneath. Above the general level rise in clumps here and there the panicled andromeda, with cluster brown fruit and the high blue berry." The andromeda Thoreau was referring to was leatherleaf, a woody shrub that persists today, still giving a reddish hue to the bogs.

During the 1800s various human activities greatly affected the Adams Woods area. From early in that century the land was frequently logged both for fuel wood and lumber. In mid-century, the Boston and Maine Railroad tracks were built. In the late nineteenth century, fires appear to have been frequent in the area.

Among the fires was one ignited by a spark from a small flame over which Thoreau and his friend Edward Hoar were cooking a fish on the shore of Fairhaven Bay. The fire raged uncontrolled until it was checked by the railroad cut at the northeast edge of the woods.

The center of the woods is high and comparatively level, but it drops off steeply into a narrow valley through the center of which runs Heywood's Brook. One hundred and fifty years ago this valley was a narrow but well-cultivated meadow, extending from beyond the present railroad embankment to Fairhaven Bay and called Pleasant Meadow. However, with the decline of farming, most of it was allowed to revert back to woodland until today only three acres of meadow remain, next to the shore of the bay.

Acquisition

The town acquired the core of the Adams Woods property, primarily from the Adams family, during 1977 through 1980. Assistance from the state's Self-Help Program, a substantial gift from the Adamses, and a major fund-raising drive made the acquisition possible. Additional contiguous pieces were added in 1986 and 1993.

Natural History

Adams Woods is a kame delta, formed by sediment deposition from meltwater flowing into glacial Lake Sudbury. Fairhaven Bay is the last vestige of that glacial lake. The deposit underfoot throughout the property is mainly sand and gravel, which washed in layers from the melting ice.

The sandy soil supports mainly a mixture of oak and white pine, and on isolated sections of the land evergreen stands have been planted: a hemlock grove on the hillside

Scott Hecker

by Heywood's Brook and three small plots of larch and Scotch pine not far from the railroad tracks. Red maple grows in areas of wetland and, by the northwest edge of Pleasant Meadow, sassafras has taken hold.

The forest within Adams Woods contains many large and mature examples of New England trees. Red, sugar, and striped maples are present as well as black, yellow, grey, and paper birches. White, red, and pin oaks are common and white ash, eastern red cedar, hemlock, American elm and pignut hickory are also well established. There is a significant stand of small chestnut, including a few flowering examples, whose seeds have been harvested in an attempt to breed blight-resistant strains. Sprinkled in amongst the forest are a few uncharacteristic tree species like European larch and Scotch pine, no doubt left over from human endeavors in the past.

Lowbush blueberry and huckleberry, the main understory shrubbery of Adams Woods, are also typical of sandy woodland situations. These grow among other ground vegetation that thrives in the dry, well-drained soil: big patches of sheep laurel and Canada mayflower, bracken fern and lady's slippers, and an occasional wildflower such as yellow loosestrife and false Solomon's seal. Additional understory plants include flowering dogwood, buttonbush, black huckleberry, wintergreen, witch hazel, sassafrass, tartarian honeysuckle, and southern arrowwood.

Among the animals that inhabit the woods are deer, raccoons, skunks, foxes and opossums. Coyotes and fishers have migrated into the area in recent times and wild turkeys have been attracted by the ample mast crop from the oaks and beeches. The most primitive of these animals is the opossum, the only marsupial of North America, which has extended its range into New England from southern states since the turn of the century. Though you are unlikely to see this solitary, nocturnal resident, which sleeps in its nest in a log, burrow, or hollow tree by day, you may find its star-like paw prints if you look on the ground.

Wetlands encircle almost the entire Adams Woods parcel. Trails run along the ridge top, and others follow lengthwise along the slopes and down past the surrounding swamps and the Fairhaven Bay floodplain. One straight path follows along Heywood's Brook, crossing the stream by a large white pine, three feet in diameter and one of the biggest in town; the brook, green with watercress in sections, flows steadily toward Fairhaven Bay.

Another trail parallels the Andromeda Ponds, serving as a vantage point from which to look at Thoreau's leatherleaf, underlain by its mat of sphagnum moss and other wetland plants—cattail, tussock sedge, and bog rosemary in flooded sections, and highbush blueberry, arrowwood, royal fern, and sensitive fern along the bank.

The ponds are nesting and feeding sites for waterfowl, and other possible sightings in the area include waterloving mammals such as muskrats and various mustelids, including mink, otter, or weasel. Muskrats are most frequently seen in spring and, though they are more active at night, in that season you may see one at any hour of the day. Watch for one swimming in the pond, its brown face and rudder-like tail showing above the water's surface.

Though the Andromeda Ponds appear ideal for muskrats, with their sloping banks for den sites and their sedges, pond weeds, and water lilies for food, they can also be a dangerous place; muskrats must beware of minks hunting in the ponds. While a grown mink is roughly the same weight as a muskrat, it is a fierce threat to the peaceful, herbivorous rodent and prefers it to any other prey.

Fairhaven Bay is host to a spectrum of waterfowl including ducks, geese, swans, and an occasional loon or great blue heron. Innumerable songbirds forage and nest in the upland portions of Adams Woods. In winter, a fluttering of wings and a whirl of chipping will indicate that a flock of species common in these woods is not far away. The mixed group of songbirds will most likely include the chickadee, the Massachusetts state bird, goldfinches, golden-crowned kinglets, red-breasted and white-breasted nuthatches, and tufted titmice, this last species having moved into Massachusetts just a half century ago, some believe in response to the increasing number of people who feed birds in the winter.

One may see blue jays eating acorns, pileated woodpeckers, which like the more remote section of forest, and during the summer months, a hermit thrush, its large brown eyes guiding it through the dim light

A solitary yet vocal bird of Adams Woods is the great crested flycatcher. Though it perches high in the tree tops, often on the same branch at the same time, day after day, the male is easy to find when it gives its loud ascending *wheep*. Great crested flycatchers nest in tree cavities, often close to wetlands or meadow edges, but there is likely only one pair breeding in this woodland because of the large territory required for this species.

One also might be fortunate enough to see a pair of ground-nesting, rufous-sided towhees on the property, though towhees are becoming scarcer. In breeding season the noisy male calls from tree limbs with his *drink-your-tea* song. When he is not staking his territory, however, a more likely place to see one of these birds is on the ground tossing up leaves and scratching in search of insects.

It is not surprising that the chipping sparrow also nests in Adams Woods because the adjacent pasture and stables to the southeast provide the horse hair that this small bird uses to line its nest. When "chippies" nest in the forest, they generally choose small clearings or openings along streams, so a likely spot for this bird's nest is beside Heywood's Brook. In summer a dawn stroll may turn up one, for this sparrow is truly an early bird, rising and beginning its morning song, a trill of chips, before any of its neighbors.

Walden Pond

General Information

Walden Pond State Reservation lies partly in Lincoln but largely in Concord. Walden Pond fills the center third of the property and is encircled by a trail that passes the site of Henry David Thoreau's famous shore-front cabin. As well as having great historical significance as Thoreau's short-term home and the subject of the author's famous book, *Walden*, the pond is popular for various recreational activities.

Swimming is allowed in Walden Pond in designated areas. Lifeguards are on duty from Memorial Day to Labor Day. The pond and surrounding paths are open daily to the public year-round from 5 a.m. to approximately one-half hour after sunset. Canoes and kayaks are allowed, and there is a special boat launch area just south of the main entrance. Dogs are prohibited at all times.

Parking

Parking is available at Walden Pond State Reservation on Route 126 for a fee. No parking is allowed on the shoulder of Route 126 or Route 2.

Links to Other Trails

Trail connections to Pine Hill and Adams Woods enable access to Lincoln and Concord conservation land.

History

Walden Pond is internationally famous because of the success of *Walden*, written by the naturalist and philosopher Henry David Thoreau of Concord, following his two-year stay by the pond from 1845 to 1847. Thoreau lived in his

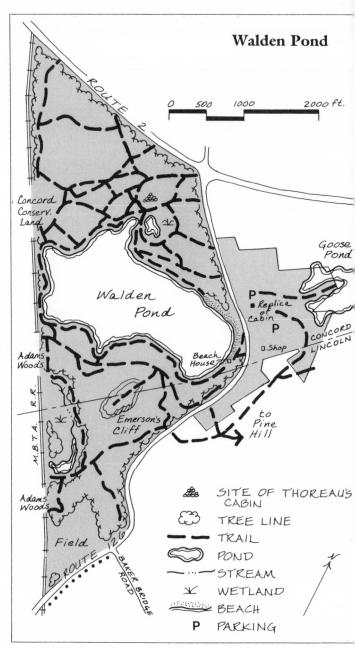

Walden Pond

0   500   1000   2000 ft.

ROUTE 2

Concord
Conserv.
Land

Goose
Pond

Walden
Pond

P
■ Replica
of Cabin

P

□ Shop

CONCORD
LINCOLN

Beach
House

Adams
Woods

M.B.T.A. R.R.

Emerson's
Cliff

to
Pine
Hill

Adams
Woods

Field

ROUTE 126

BAKER BRIDGE
ROAD

🐝 SITE OF THOREAU'S
      CABIN

☁ TREE LINE

▬ ▬ ▬ TRAIL

⬭ POND

····· STREAM

⤳ WETLAND

⋯⋯ BEACH

P PARKING

cabin by the pond through the generosity of his neighbor and mentor, Ralph Waldo Emerson, who offered him the use of his woodlot there. Emerson also introduced Thoreau to other authors and thinkers of that time, including Ellery Channing, Bronson Alcott, Margaret Fuller, and Nathaniel Hawthorne.

Thoreau began planning and constructing his one-room cabin in March 1845. By midsummer he was ready to take up residence and on July 4, 1845, he began his experiment: two years spent writing, studying nature, gardening, and reading, as well as entertaining guests at the pond and making frequent visits to friends in Concord. Nine years later, in 1854, Thoreau had published the record of his experience, entitled *Walden, or Life in the Woods*. Since then it has never been out of print.

In 1866, just four years after Thoreau died, the Fitchburg Railroad built an excursion park on Ice Fort Cove at the southwestern side of Walden, which people reached easily by train from Boston and Waltham and points farther west. Concessions, swings, bathhouses, halls for social gatherings, and later a track and baseball diamond were among the attractions; but when the park burned in 1902, it was never rebuilt. Nevertheless, the pond has continually remained a popular attraction.

Acquisition

In 1922 the Heywood, Forbes, and Emerson families gave 80 acres, including Walden Pond, to the state. Their purpose in donating the land was for "preserving the Walden of Emerson and Thoreau, its shores and nearby woodlands, for the public who wish to enjoy the pond, the woods and nature, including bathing, boating, fishing, and picnicking."

Natural History

The sandy soil of the Walden land was brought southward by the meltwater streams from the receding glacier 10,000 years ago. The pond itself is a kettlehole left by an immense ice block that created a deep depression in the ground. Over 100 feet deep and encompassing over six acres, Walden is technically a lake rather than a pond. Thoreau, who often worked as a surveyor, measured the depth with a stone on a string. His calculations match those determined with modern-day equipment.

The land where Thoreau chose to build his cabin had been logged just 15 years before, so new growth surrounded his dwelling. He wrote, "My house was on the side of a hill, immediately on the edge of the larger wood, in the midst of a young forest of pitch pines and hickories. . . . In my front yard grew the strawberry, black berry, and life everlasting, johnswort and goldenrod, shrub oaks and sand cherry, blueberry and groundnut." Beyond Thoreau's open "sprout lands," the pond was "a perennial spring in the midst of a pine and oak woods," one of the

Scott Hecker

few remaining woodlands at that time because most had been cleared for farming.

By 1922, when Walden Pond and the adjacent property became park land, most of the woods had been cleared, but today the pine-oak forest has returned. Pitch pines once again form a grove alongside the site of Thoreau's cabin and, as before, highbush blueberries grow at the edge of the pond. On the south side of the pond, hemlocks shade the water, and shadbush fills in sections with dappled light, as do some of the pretty woodland flowers, including pink lady's slipper, birdfoot violet, wood anemone, and sarsaparilla.

Much of the wildlife that Thoreau encountered is still present at Walden Pond, "the fox, and skunk, and rabbit," as well as squirrels, chipmunks, raccoons, and many of the bird species Thoreau described, such as kingfishers, red-tailed hawks, and chickadees.

Suggested Walk: Around the Pond

The most popular walk is the trail that circles the pond, which you may follow in either direction. It starts at the bottom of the path from Route 126 and is close to the shoreline the entire way around. As you proceed, you can choose at many points to walk in the woods or by the water, as the beach extends along much of the shore, depending on the water level. Because of the extremely high use of the area, no dogs are allowed, and fences have been erected in many places to prevent the trampling of plants between the shore and the path. Although this is not a welcome or attractive feature, the fencing has been remarkably effective in helping the vegetation to recover and in preventing further erosion of the hillsides.

To reach the site of Thoreau's cabin, begin the walk by turning right at the edge of the pond. The path follows the northeastern edge of the pond to the little cove where there is a sign directing you up a well-worn path into the woods. Nothing remains now of his original cabin. To commemorate the site, a pile of rocks has been building over the years, and each hiker/visitor is welcome to bring a stone or two to add to the pile. As you look back to the water from the cabin site, try to imagine the scene as it was in Thoreau's time, recently timbered and just beginning to return to forest; there were small trees and many sun-loving flowers here. He lived at the edge of the forest rather than within it.

As you continue around to the far side of the pond, farthest from Route 126, the shore is close to the railroad line between Fitchburg, Concord, and Boston, which existed in Thoreau's time. It is hard to imagine that for thirty-six years in the late 1800s, an amusement park dominated this lovely cove, where thousands of people came to picnic, swim, dance, and enjoy the country air. However, the beaches in this area are now some of the most quiet places along the pond edge, good for fishing, swimming, and pic-nicking. To complete your walk, continue along the edge of the pond, enjoying the history, the scenery, the clear deep waters and the peacefulness, even if there are many others around you. The path will lead you back to the beach area, where you can return to your car or continue to explore other trails.

There is a veritable maze of trails farther back from the pond, especially on the north side, as indicated on the map in this book. You can also pick up a Trail Map of the area published by the Massachusetts Forest and Park Service which shows the area in more detail. However, because the maps are confusing in many places, (with few or no signs) perhaps it is best to wander along the paths and enjoy the area, without having to know exactly which trail you are following. As the area is confined by Routes 2 and 126, the water, and the railroad tracks, you cannot get lost!

When you return to your car, be sure to notice the rep-lica of Thoreau's cabin, on the opposite side of Route 126, which is often open to visitors, and the wonderful statue of this remarkable man. In any case, this is an area to return to in all seasons, a real treasure for both first-time visitors and local residents.

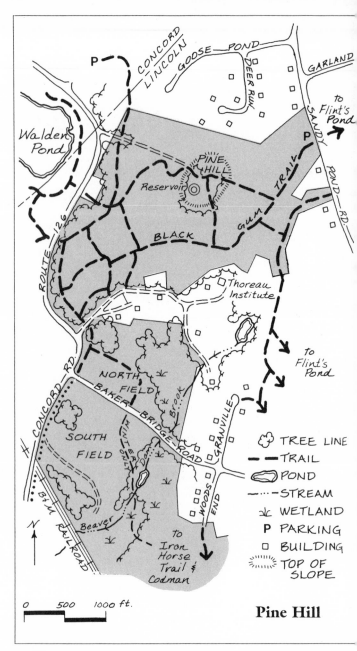

Pine Hill

TREE LINE
TRAIL
POND
STREAM
WETLAND
P PARKING
BUILDING
TOP OF SLOPE

0   500   1000 ft.

N

Pine Hill

General Information

Most of this hundred-acre property is a dry hillside with a second-growth oak and pine forest, but the highlight of the area is the view from the Concord reservoir on the summit. On fair days Mount Monadnock and Mount Wachusett are visible to the northwest and west, respectively. Bikes may be ridden on the main Pine Hill Loop Trail along the southern grade, joining Black Gum trail to Sandy Pond Road. Blue and white markers identify these trails.

Parking

Parking is available at Walden Pond State Reservation on Route 126 for a fee. A few parking spots are also available on the shoulder along Sandy Pond Road, about 50 feet from the trail head. Be sure not to block the gateway for rescue vehicles.

Links to Other Trails

The Pine Hill trails connect with Flint's Pond, Walden Pond, and Baker Bridge North. A town bicycle trail crosses Baker Bridge Rd where it meets Route 126 and is located at the southwestern edge of the Pine Hill trail network. This part of the trail is part of the Bay Circuit Trail, marked by vertical white rectangles.

History

The Pine Hill land was part of a grant to the Billing family from the Town of Concord in the 1600s, and it remained in their ownership until 1762 when John Billing, Jr. sold it to James Miles. The property changed hands several times in the nineteenth century. Thoreau knew the area and described the beech grove and Beech Spring at the foot of Pine Hill in his *Journal*. But the most illustrious owner lived on Pine Hill in the early part of the twentieth century. Henry Lee Higginson bought the property for his son Alexander, a renowned sportsman, steeplechase rider, and author, and built in addition to his main house, a stable, kennels, and housing for professional help. Alexander laid out a steeplechase course, presented annual horse shows, and was Master of Hounds for The Middlesex Hunt. According to J. Quincy Adams, a fellow horseman and Lincoln resident, "[Higginson] added much color to the town from 1900 to the Great War, and after the war [he] moved to England, where he continued his hunting activities." Higginson once said that he had to give up fox hunting in Lincoln because "the American motorist, unlike his English cousin, is not trained to stop for hounds on the highway."

Natural History

Currently, Pine Hill would more appropriately be called Oak Hill because the forest is a mixture of red, white, and black oak, except for sections of white pine on the western slope and patches of pine just beyond seedling stage here and there. During the aftermath of the last ice age, when glacial Lake Sudbury covered most of the area, the hill was an island. Now the wooded hill is encircled and crisscrossed by trails and capped by a grassy field that covers an underground reservoir.

Suggested Walk: From Sandy Pond Road to the top of the reservoir, around the back side, and back to Sandy Pond Road.

Park at the trail junction on Sandy Pond Road south of Garland Road, then follow the wide trail into the woods on the west side of Sandy Pond Road. Before reaching the dry, wooded hillside, the path crosses a low, damp area with many highbush blueberries, several small red maples, lowbush blueberries, cinnamon and wood ferns. Note the mossy bases on the shadier north sides of trees in this section.

As the trail begins to climb, it enters an oak woodland that covers much of the parcel. Here most of the vegetation is new growth, including sassafras and a significant number of chestnut saplings, although their future is bleak. This area has been significantly altered by heavy logging in the nineteenth century, damage from the hurricane of 1938, and the devastation caused by fires, gypsy moths, and carpenter ants. Along the trail, also, are goldenrod, lowbush blueberry, sweet fern, bracken, and the occasional pink lady's slipper.

At the first trail intersection, a right onto the Pine Hill Loop leads to an open hilltop with a multitude of pasture

flowers such as black-eyed Susan, red clover, daisies, cow vetch, and Queen Anne's lace. From the summit, the vista, overlooking Walden Pond towards the far horizon, is framed on either side by white birches, which often have chickadees feeding in the twigs in winter.

In his *Journal* on May 17, 1858, Thoreau remarked on the sights from atop the hill, which he alternately called Bare Hill or Bear Hill: "I thought yesterday that the view of the mountains from the bare hill on the Lincoln side of Flint's Pond was very grand. Surely they do not look so grand anywhere within twenty miles of them. . . . I doubt if in the landscape there can be anything finer than a distant mountain-range. They are a constant elevating influence."

The Pine Hill Loop, marked with yellow discs, continues on the northwestern side of the reservoir, near the maintenance road, and switches back down the hill. On this incline, the land is dotted with a few huge rocks, called erratics, brought to their present sites by the last glacier. You can walk over the top or around the hill to the maintenance road and continue down this road a short distance to the point where the trail goes off to the left.

At the junction of three trails, bear to the left and enter a wide trail, with a base of coal cinders laid when burning coal was a common way to heat homes. From this trail a path heads off to the left through a varied woodland of oak, black birch, and some large white pines.

A number of songbirds feed in the more amply wooded portions of Pine Hill. The hermit thrush, the only New England thrush with a cinnamon-colored tail, and the ovenbird sometimes rustle among the leaves on the forest floor, while the rose-breasted grosbeak and scarlet tanager frequent the canopy above. Scarlet tanagers have long been abundant in the woodlands surrounding Pine Hill. In the nineteenth century ornithologist William Brewster recorded that they were "very abundant." Winter birds of this area climb along the trunks looking for insects: hairy and downy woodpeckers, white-breasted nuthatches, and well-camouflaged brown creepers. The brown creeper's unique behavior is illustrated by its repeat performance of spiraling up one tree and flying to the base of the next.

At the next trail junction, an old stone foundation is all that remains of a former ice house. It is likely that the building stored ice harvested from nearby ponds such as Flint's Pond, Beaver Pond, and Fairhaven Bay. The ice house was abandoned many years ago and subsequently razed by the fire department. Virginia day flower, mosses, and poor man's pepper cover the wall, and, just beyond the foundation on the right, a large patch of pipsissewa blankets the ground under the oaks. The trail then skirts the edge of Pine Hill and leads back to Sandy Pond Road. Various animal signs may be evident along this path: rectangular holes chiseled in old snags by pileated woodpeckers, and footprints and scat left by red fox, skunk, raccoon, deer, or coyote. The trail takes a final 45-degree bend to the left and emerges on Sandy Pond Road.

Flint's Pond

General Information

One of the most prominent features of Lincoln's landscape, Flint's Pond serves as the major supply of the town's drinking water. Most of the land abutting the 156-acre pond is in conservation, totaling over 200 acres, including the grounds of the DeCordova Museum. A network of walking, skiing, and riding trails circles the pond. Because Flint's Pond is a reservoir, no swimming, fishing, boating, or wading is allowed, and all trails leading to the water's edge have been closed. Dogs must be controlled and kept far away from the water. Town conservation rangers patrol this area frequently and ticket offenders.

Parking

Parking is available for a fee (no fee for Lincoln residents) in the lower parking lot at the DeCordova Museum except during special events, as well as at the Brooks School behind the gym. The trail to the pond from the school is about three-quarters of a mile long. Additional parking is available south of Garland Road by Gates 23 and 24 on Sandy Pond Road. Please obey the "No Parking" signs by the pond and along Sandy Pond Road, and be sure not to block gates.

Links to Other Trails

The Flint's Pond trails connect with trails of the Pine Hill, Wheeler Farm, Tanner's Brook, and Schools to Codman Bridge conservation areas.

History

Before the arrival of European settlers, the area around Flint's Pond was frequented by members of the Musketaquid tribe, who lived nearby along the Concord River. They gathered chestnuts and fruits and hunted wild turkey, deer and other animals. Fish were abundant in the pond. Later, only a decade or so after the first colonists started villages in New England, families received allotments near the pond to balance their holdings—meadows for hay, upland for orchards, pastureland for grazing, and woodlots for fuel and lumber.

In the 1650s a ditch leading away from the pond, which is still visible on the north shore, was used to carry water to Concord in what was then called Sawmill Brook. The water serviced grist mills and sawmills in the area.

Flint's Pond was included in a royal grant of 750 acres to Thomas Flint in the 1640s. Other early abutters were the Brooks and Bulkeley families. In 1778, Zachariah Smith purchased a large parcel next to the pond. His family planted orchards of cherry, apple, pear, and quince trees along the west and north shores of the pond and marketed the fruit in the Boston area.

Zachariah's descendent, Charles Sumner Smith, expanded these holdings in the early 1890s, particularly along the western and northern sides of the pond and in the Pine Hill area. He built a cabin of chestnut wood harvested after the chestnut blight, which occurred close to the turn of the century and killed the mature chestnuts surrounding the pond. The chimney of the cabin, which still stands, was beautifully constructed from odd-shaped stones and water-cut rocks. The cabin was used for recreational purposes with family and friends for a number of years, and later the Lincoln Boy Scouts were allowed to use it until a fire destroyed it in the 1970s.

The pond was a popular place for boating. At the end of the eighteenth century, John Codman of Boston kept his large boat on the pond. Scholars of the Liberal School, founded in Lincoln in the 1790s, used the boat, which was large enough to carry 15 to 20 people. In about 1800, Jonas

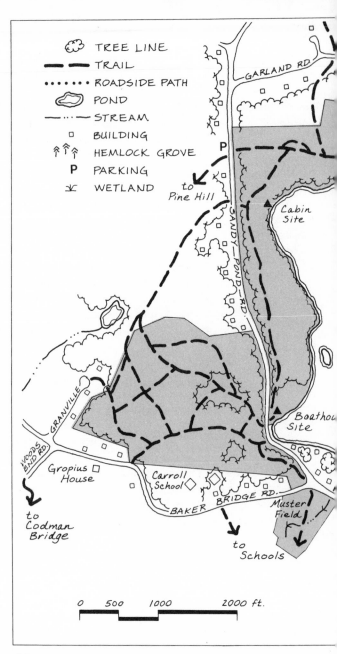

LEGEND

🌳 TREE LINE
— — TRAIL
••••• ROADSIDE PATH
🌊 POND
—··— STREAM
□ BUILDING
🌲🌲🌲 HEMLOCK GROVE
P PARKING
☇ WETLAND

GARLAND RD.

P

to
Pine Hill

SANDY POND RD.

Cabin
Site

GRANVILLE

WOODS END RD.

Gropius □
House

Carroll
School ◇

BAKER BRIDGE RD.

Boathouse
Site

Muster
Field

to
Codman
Bridge

to
Schools

0   500   1000   2000 ft.

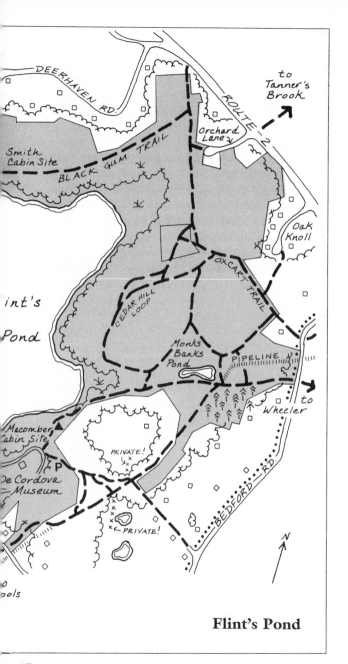

Flint's Pond

Smith described it: "This boat when on the water and at a distance from the shore made a beautiful appearance."

In 1874 the towns of Concord and Lincoln began using Flint's Pond as a public water supply. Concord drew water from the pond until the late 1970s. Today Flint's Pond serves as a primary source of water for the town of Lincoln.

Julian DeCordova and his wife, Mary Elizabeth Dana, purchased land for an estate on the southeast shore of Flint's Pond in the 1880s. Two years later they built a brown shingle summer house and, in 1910, they added a northern French-style castle, landscaped with rolling lawns and curving walks. DeCordova, a wealthy businessman who traveled extensively in foreign countries, brought back "everything that took [his] fancy in every part of the world." In 1930 he gave the resulting collection, along with the entire estate, to the town, though most of his collection is no longer at the DeCordova Museum which focuses today on New England artists.

In the 1890s the Lincoln Boat Club built a boathouse on the southwestern shore across from the present pumphouse, complete with a dance hall on the second floor. Then in 1910, the club constructed an ice house in the back. Several times in winter, due to damage from ice, the boathouse had to be moved. Later, nature having taken its toll, the building was abandoned and eventually removed by the town.

Several other small structures were built along the edge of the pond in the 1930s. Nothing remains of a cabin built by Garland along the western shore of the pond, but there is still an assortment of debris on the northwest side, including a staircase that was apparently part of a cabin constructed by fishermen.

The pond's original name, Flint's Pond, after Thomas Flint, was reinstated at the Lincoln Town Meeting in 1986. Until then it was known as Sandy Pond, and a hundred years before that as Forest Lake.

Acquisition

The first acquisition of conservation land on Flint's Pond was initiated in 1958 when a parcel of land along the western shores of the pond became available for development. Concerned about the town's drinking water supply and the aesthetic impacts of development, several citizens founded the Lincoln Land Conservation Trust specifically for the acquisition of a parcel of this watershed land.

Although it was generally felt in Lincoln that land around the pond should not be developed, many years were required to secure the land for conservation. The last large parcels bordering the pond were acquired in 1984 when the town purchased 125 acres from the Sandy Pond Trust, a private trust of the Smith family.

Natural History

Thoreau first chose a section of the Flint's Pond shoreline as the place to build his cabin. Tradition says, however, that permission was denied by Captain Ephraim Flint, who owned the pond and the site Thoreau desired, and who had doubtless heard about the extensive accidental forest fire Thoreau had set by Fairhaven Bay. Whatever the reason for Flint's refusal, Thoreau was forced to settle on Walden Pond, but the famous naturalist's preference for Flint's Pond is a tribute to its wild beauty.

Like Thoreau, who frequently circuited the pond with various companions in the mid-1800s, present-day visitors walking the protected watershed land will encounter a wide variety of trees, shrubs, and birds along the trails.

In spring and fall, many migrating warblers scout for insects in the trees and shrubbery. The palm warbler, an early spring arrival, bobs its tail as it forages close to the ground, and in May mixed flocks, including yellow-rumped, black-throated green, and magnolia warblers, flit among the tree tops as they stop to feed on their way north. In summer a pair of eastern phoebes often nests in the deciduous forestland near the Smith cabin site on the northern shore. This waterfront haunt, with an abundant population of flying insects, is ideal for raising and feeding their young.

Ducks also stop here during migration, especially greater scaup, black ducks, buffleheads, and golden-eyes, and there are the usual flocks of Canada geese and the occasional snow goose or cormorant. Wood ducks have nested here in the past, finding large dead trees very suitable for their nests if they are lucky enough to find an available hole, already excavated.

At one time there appear to have been two islands in Flint's Pond. In a description of the pond written by Jonas Smith around 1800, a half-acre island was called Rocky Island and another three-acre island was named Bushy Island, which is probably the one visible today.

Suggested Walk: the trails along the north and western sides of the pond, accessible from Sandy Pond Road.

If you park at the largest and most northerly area on Sandy Pond Road, you will see the wide trail just south of Garland Road, called the Black Gum Trail. This trail is open to bicyclists and horseback riders as well as hikers, and is so marked: yellow discs for hikers and blue diamond markers for bikers. (Red diamonds indicate that bikes are prohibited.) The wide, fairly straight trail goes across the north side of the pond and is a beautiful, peaceful wood road where two people can easily walk side by side, not common on the Lincoln trails.

This lovely trail hums with avian activity in the spring and early summer: cardinals, titmice, blue jays, vireos and some warblers are all busy raising young here in the treetops and shrubbery, calling to each other, declaring their territories, and later, bringing food to their young. You will first be in a forest of tall oaks which give way to large hemlocks in the damper places. There are various junctions with other more narrow trails which you can take to explore more of the area. However, note that all trails leading directly to the pond shore have been blocked by fences and signs to protect the water quality, as it is a source of drinking water for the town. This was mandated by state regulations. Continue along this trail, enjoying the peace and quiet, and the sense of others having lived here in colonial times. There are stone walls on both sides, indicating that there were farms here in the eighteenth and nineteenth centuries. On your left as you head away from Sandy Pond Road, midway along the northern shore, you can find the remains of the old chimney of the Smith cabin.

After about fifteen minutes, you will approach Route 2, evident as traffic noise increases dramatically. You cross over two small bridges and soon after, the trail turns to the right (south) where it becomes the Oxcart Trail. The Oxcart Trail closely resembles the Black Gum Trail, except that poison ivy thrives here and encroaches on both sides of the path along much of its length. (Leaves of three: Let it be.) There are many forks in the trail and if you take each right hand fork, you will follow the "Cedar Hill Loop," in a counterclockwise direction and be as close to the pond as possible, where there are occasional views of the water from an elevated vantage point. You will also pass two patches of magnificent hemlocks, one on either side of the trail, towering 50 to 90 feet high and shading the areas underneath, where there is little vegetation on the smooth needle-covered ground.

Most of the drier land on this side of Flint's Pond is dominated by oaks, interspersed with pine, sweet birch, hickory, beech, and hemlock. The wetter portions, nearer the pond, support species such as winterberry, swamp azalea, high-bush blueberry, and tupelo. Tupelo, or black gum, is a unique tree with berries eaten by birds and mammals and bright red foliage in autumn.

You can continue along here, to the stone monument in honor of a young woman, Aureet Bar-Yam, who drowned in 1991 while attempting to rescue her dog which had fallen through the ice. At this point you can turn around or continue in a counterclockwise direction circling back to the Oxcart and Black Gum Trails where the view will be remarkably different seen from the opposite direction.

If you choose to explore the western side of the pond, the narrow section between the pond and Sandy Pond Road, turn right off the Black Gum trail at the first intersection and head south. With the pond on your left, you will be on a narrow path, located halfway between the pond and the road that runs through a lovely patch of woods. This is a pleasant area with easy access from the road. The woods are open here, allowing several good views of the pond. The tallest trees are entirely deciduous, mostly black oaks, with young white pines in the understory. It is easy to imagine how this section of forest will change in the next twenty or thirty years, strongly influenced by the large numbers of deer who prefer to munch on oak seedlings rather than young pines, so that very few young oaks can survive to reach ten or fifteen feet. Look around: do you see any midsized oaks?

This trail ends by a large meadow at the southwestern side of the pond, where the pond and road are close together and there is a pleasant view of the pond across an overgrown meadow, which the town maintains with annual mowings. From here, you will need to retrace your steps back to your car or loop back through the Pine Hill trails.

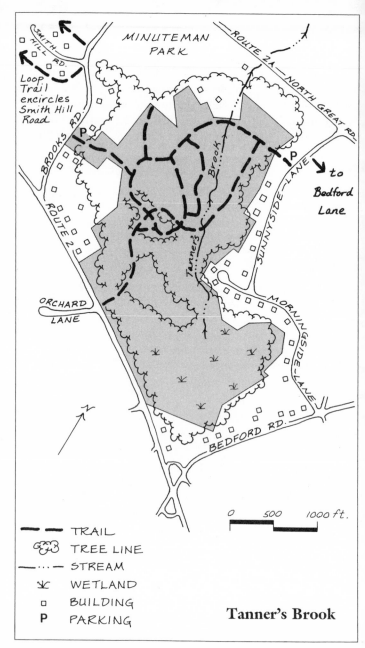

MINUTEMAN PARK

SMITH HILL RD.

ROUTE 2A — NORTH GREAT RD.

Loop Trail encircles Smith Hill Road

BROOKS RD.

ROUTE 2

P

P

to Bedford Lane

Tanner's Brook

ORCHARD LANE

SUNNYSIDE LANE

MORNINGSIDE LANE

BEDFORD RD.

N

0   500   1000 ft.

— — — TRAIL

TREE LINE

— · · — STREAM

WETLAND

BUILDING

P PARKING

Tanner's Brook

7
Tanner's Brook

General Information

The Tanner's Brook land north of Route 2 includes about 110 acres of woods and swamps, with wide cart tracks and narrow trails winding through the parcel.

Parking

Parking for one or two cars is available on Brooks Road where a trail leads into the conservation land. Limited parking is also possible on the shoulder of Sunnyside Lane by the entrance to the trail. No parking is permitted along Route 2.

Links to Other Trails

Crossing Sunnyside Lane, one can access the trails near Bedford Lane and from there cross Route 2A to Minuteman National Historic Park.

History

Tanner's Brook was originally part of the Brooks family farm. The Brookses were tanners and used the stream that runs through the middle of this parcel for soaking hides. A tanyard on this stream, called Elm or Tanner's Brook, was located on the far side of Route 2A and operated from the late seventeenth to mid-eighteenth century.

Natural History

Tanner's Brook, a lovely sand and gravel-bottomed stream with mossy stones along its bank, runs north through a moist woodland with an open canopy, described by a local naturalist as "close and leafy and positively joyous in springtime." In that season, he says, "The woods ring with song."

From a broad wood-chip path, observers can hear—and sometimes see—migrant warblers and warm-weather song-birds such as wood thrushes on the forest floor and scarlet tanagers among the tall, shimmery-barked yellow birches and the oaks and red maples of the wet lowland. Listen for the wood thrush, which is drawn to this swampy world of soggy stumps, lush fern growth, and purple skunk cabbage shoots. Many say that this robin-like thrush, rusty above and white speckled with black below, has a song une-qualled by any other forest bird except its close relative, the hermit thrush.

Blue-winged warblers, broad-winged hawks, and ruffed grouse have all nested in the Tanner's Brook woods, and it's likely that they still do. The blue-winged warbler is found in pastures which are in an early stage of growing into forest. This type of habitat is disappearing as woods continue to mature, and thus the number of blue-winged warblers is diminishing. This shy warbler is more easily heard than seen; the male will perch on a high branch and show off his bright yellow and blue-grey plumage while singing his distinctive *beee-buzzzz* song.

If you walk the parcel in winter, the forest is quieter than in summer, but on a cold day in January the chickadees may already be practicing their two-note *fee-bee* courting call. As spring approaches, listen for the cardinals' *cheer, cheer, cheer* and the *Peter, Peter, Peter* song of tufted tit-mice.

The southern section of the Tanner's Brook parcel con-sists of sands and gravel. A large gravel pit, now covered by pines, grasses, and other plants, is still evident through the vegetation which indicates that portions were scraped and excavated in the past. More of the typical upland trees, such as oak and white pine, predominate in this upland portion of the property. Look also for small beeches, with

their smooth, light-gray bark and papery brown leaves in winter, while the red cedar and grey birch hint that the land was formerly pasture. Longtime Lincoln residents will remember the neighborhood ball field next to Route 2. This area has reverted to a meadow with remnants of the old asparagus field still evident, along with other flower-garden favorites such as some daffodils and a patch of periwinkle.

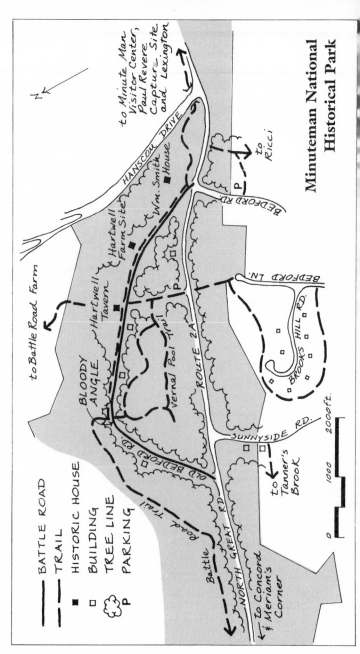

Minuteman National Historical Park

BATTLE ROAD
TRAIL
HISTORIC HOUSE
BUILDING
TREE LINE
PARKING

to Minute Man Visitor Center, Paul Revere Capture Site and Lexington

HANSCOM DRIVE

Wm. Smith House

Hartwell Farm Site

to Battle Road Farm

Hartwell Tavern

BLOODY ANGLE

Vernal Pool Trail

BEDFORD RD.

to Ricci

BEDFORD LN.

HILL RD.

BROOKS

ROUTE 2A

OLD BEDFORD RD.

Battle Road Trail

NORTH GREAT RD.

to Concord & Meriam's Corner

SUNNYSIDE RD.

to Tanner's Brook

0   1000   2000 ft.

N

Minuteman National Historical Park

General Information

Minuteman National Historical Park, flanking Battle Road where the Minutemen first took up arms, in Concord, Lincoln, and Lexington, preserves buildings and land associated with the beginning of the American Revolution. About a third of the park's 750 acres of land lies within the town of Lincoln. The Minute Man Visitor Center is on Route 2A in Lexington, about half a mile east of the Lincoln town line, and has numerous displays, programs, and a gift shop.

The historic sites in Lincoln include the colonial William Smith House and Ephraim Hartwell Tavern; the ruins of the Samuel Hartwell House; the Bloody Angle, where some of the heaviest fighting of the first day occurred; and the site of Paul Revere's capture by the redcoats. Please contact Minuteman National Historical Park at (978) 369–6993 or www.nps.gov/mima for information on dates and times of opening and a listing of programs involving the Lincoln sites.

Parking

There are several parking areas at historic sites along Route 2A, where informational displays are provided.

History

The events along the Battle Road in Lincoln, in which over seventy-four men are known to have participated, began around one or two in the morning on April 19, 1775. Spring had come early that year. In the moonlight, the white blooms of the apple trees were visible. The first British patrol had already passed through the night before and was hidden in a field nearby. Paul Revere had ridden out from Boston and was now on his way to Concord after joining Major William Dawes in Lexington. Soon another late night rider, Dr. Samuel Prescott, overtook them. A young Concordian and "high son of Liberty", who had been out late courting, Prescott joined Revere and Dawes. As they approached the Lincoln line, Prescott and Dawes fell behind to rouse a household. Suddenly two mounted officers appeared from beneath a tree and captured Revere. Still lagging behind, Dawes and Prescott were able to evade capture. Dawes turned quickly and galloped back up the road. Prescott, an excellent horseman, jumped a stone wall and maneuvered through wood and swamp to a nearby house. Both were able to continue Revere's mission and spread the warning.

Later that morning, Mary Hartwell, wife of Sergeant Samuel Hartwell of the Lincoln Minutemen, heard the British regulars before she saw them. She was quite impressed with the bright red line of British Grenadiers and light infantry as they marched past her home toward Concord.

The regulars retreated down the same route they had come. When they reached Meriam's Corner, they were slowed further by the small bridge crossing Mill Brook. Meanwhile, the minutemen hastened across Great Meadows and down Bedford Road. Reinforcements came and others arrived from the south. As the British passed over the small bridge, a crash of musketry erupted. The running fight had begun. Just inside the Lincoln line, where the old road turns sharply north, it is bordered by stone walls and is slightly sunken below the surrounding terrain. Operating independently or in small militia units, the minutemen were able to run ahead through field and orchard and take cover behind trees and walls. As the redcoats got closer, they were again met by a barrage of fire. Eight were left dead or dying as the retreating British marched on. This stretch of road has been called the Bloody Angle ever since.

The following morning Mary Hartwell was on her way to visit her father, Ephraim Flint, when she came upon a cart driven by two elderly neighbors; in the cart were the dead soldiers. She followed the cart as it creaked slowly on and past the Flint homestead to the burying ground. There, on a little knoll apart from where the town's founders were buried, the two men buried the soldiers in an unmarked grave. Over a century later a simple monument was erected by Lincoln citizens in what is now called the Precinct Burying Ground.

Natural History

Minuteman National Historical Park land is made up of deciduous forest, abandoned hayfields and orchards, wetlands, rivers, ponds, and miles of stone walls, all of which provide habitat for the many birds and mammals of the area. Among the most notable mammals are white-tailed deer, coyotes, cottontails, skunks, opossums, and raccoons. A combination of native plants and many exotic species can be found throughout the property, evidence of centuries of intensive human influence on the land.

Suggested Walk: Loop walk along the Vernal Pool Trail, starting near the Hartwell Tavern and returning along the Battle Road Trail

Park in the Hartwell Tavern lot on Route 2A and follow the path towards the tavern. Shortly before reaching the main Battle Road Trail, turn left through a break in the stone wall onto the Vernal Pool Trail. The trail passes through open deciduous woodland and just before it enters the deeper woods, note the tangle of wild grape and bittersweet vines on the left entwining the trees. Jack-in-the-pulpit can be found along the woodland path, as well as the ubiquitous poison ivy, sometimes growing low to the ground and sometimes encircling tree trunks with hairy vines. Clubmoss and Canada mayflower carpet the forest floor. On a summer day listen for the crescendoing *teacher, teacher, teacher* song of the oven bird, more likely to be heard than seen, and the high *pee-a-wee* call of the

wood pewee. After going through an area of young white pines, the trail crosses a stream and comes to a junction. A turn to the left leads along a rocky path to a boardwalk and observation deck overlooking the vernal "pool", now growing in with shrubs and maples. On an early April day this is the place to hear a chorus of spring peepers, which are tiny tree frogs only one inch long, and wood frogs, which sound very similar to quacking ducks. From the deck in the summer, listen for the banjo-like *glunk* of green frogs and observe various wetland-loving shrubs such as buttonbush, white swamp azalea, and highbush blueberry. A right turn from the trail junction leads across another boardwalk over the wetland and on into the woods, where in the summer one can see masses of white leafless Indian pipes poking up from rotting leaves and logs. These plants are unusual in that they lack chlorophyll and thus do not gain nutrients from the reaction of sunlight with chlorophyll. Instead, they gain sustenance from a parasitic relationship with a fungus around their roots which breaks down organic matter in the decomposing vegetation.

The trail continues through the woods and opens onto the Battle Road Trail, where a turn to the left leads almost at once to the Bloody Angle. A right turn leads back to the Hartwell Tavern. Approaching the Tavern, note the black locust trees on the left and a young catalpa tree on the right, recognized by its broad leaves and white tubular flowers in June and July, and long brown seed pods in the fall.

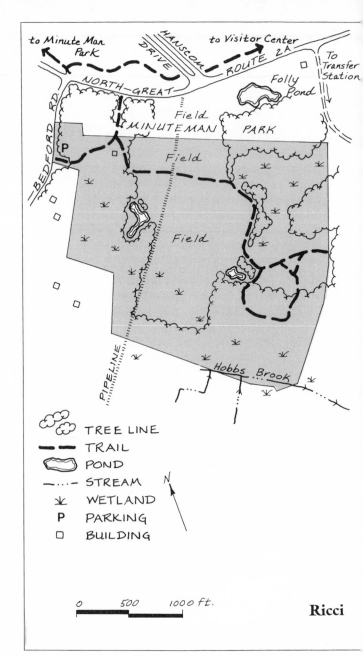

to Minute Man Park

to Visitor Center

HANSCOM DRIVE

ROUTE 2A

To Transfer Station

NORTH GREAT

BEDFORD RD.

Folly Pond

Field

MINUTEMAN

PARK

P

Field

Field

PIPELINE

Hobbs Brook

             TREE LINE
— — —   TRAIL
            POND
—···—   STREAM
  ✦   WETLAND
  P   PARKING
  □   BUILDING

N

0   500   1000 ft.

Ricci

Ricci

General Information

The Ricci conservation land consists of 94 acres of agricultural fields, young woods, and a swamp. In a leisurely one or two-hour walk, a hiker passes through all the habitats. For birdwatchers, the open areas are particularly good places for seeing songbirds.

Parking

Limited parking is available on the shoulder on the east side of Bedford Road near the conservation land sign, which marks the trail entrance.

Links to other Trails

Across Route 2A to the north one can access Minuteman National Historical Park's Battle Road Trail, which passes through a tunnel under Hanscom Drive.

History

A broad expanse of wet meadow in North Lincoln, the Ricci parcel has been used for agriculture since the 1700s. Over the centuries, hay, corn, flax, rye, barley, and hemp have been among the most successful crops, and up until the mid-1700s, swamp joint grass, a plant that grew naturally in the wetlands, was harvested as winter hay for cattle and horses. Using a series of dams and ditches, farmers maintained a water level in the wet meadow that favored this native grass.

In the 1700s, this section of land belonged to the Whittimore Farm; then, in 1791, Joel Whittimore sold 50 acres, together with a house and barn, to Aaron Brooks. Added to the adjoining Brooks land, the farm eventually reached a size of 125 acres.

One of Aaron Brooks's six children, Thomas, continued to live there and farm the land until 1888, when he sold the place to Abbie E. Bean of Lincoln. Bean's family retained the land for 75 years, finally selling the farm to the Ricci family of Lexington. The Riccis grew vegetables on the property for two decades for the local market until the town of Lincoln purchased the farmland and surrounding acreage in 1983. To this day, the area is under cultivation; the town leases the fields to a local farmer who grows corn in the rich, sandy loam.

Natural History

In addition to the fields still in cultivation, the Ricci conservation land includes sections of farmland that have been recently stripped of topsoil, cut over, or abandoned. These upland sections are interspersed with ponds, ditches, and expanses of red maple swamp. The transition from one habitat to another, and one successional stage to the next, makes the Ricci land an interesting parcel from a botanical and wildlife perspective. Grasses and wildflowers fill the abandoned meadows, attracting goldfinches, indigo buntings, and song sparrows that feed on the seeds and nest along the protective bordering thickets. Many colors of flowers bloom in the meadows: yellow evening primrose, white boneset, pink Joe-Pye weed, violet aster, and rusty dock, to name a few. Rimming the large planted field are early successional trees such as gray birch, smooth and staghorn sumac, chokecherry, and quaking aspen. Wildlife is abundant in and around this large field. Tracks of coyotes, foxes, and deer, and more recently fishers, are often present in the dirt or snow cover, and a fortunate observer can get a look at one of these mammals as it hunts or browses in the area.

Birdwatchers have sighted many hawks and songbirds that frequent this habitat. Brown thrashers nest in dense shrubbery near the field, the male employing his large song repertoire to announce his presence and attract a female. Migrating sharp-shinned hawks and merlin falcons seek perches at the field edge where they watch for small birds feeding on the ground.

Other noteworthy songbirds seen on the Ricci fields are grasshopper sparrows. In winter, horned larks frequently scurry among the furrows of the field, although good camouflage makes them hard to spot. The horned lark, a distinctive little sprite of wide-open spaces, walks swiftly with long strides as it makes the rounds of its territory. This bird, once called the snow lark, is unmistakable because of the two black tufts on its head for which it is named. Originally, the horned lark was a prairie species, but its range expanded eastward in the nineteenth century as it adopted farm fields as habitat. Tree sparrows are regular winter visitors here, and snow buntings and redpolls appear occasionally.

Another species associated with this sort of agricultural land, the water pipit, frequently visits these fields during fall migration, perhaps stopping near puddles in the field.

Though hard to distinguish from the various brown field sparrows, pipits are walkers, not hoppers, and their constantly teetering tails are an identifying feature.

Most of the wetlands to the east of the farm fields are filled with woody plants such as red maple, elderberry, winterberry (a deciduous holly), and highbush blueberry. In this swampy area near Hobbs Brook, groups of spring peepers—tiny light brown tree frogs that are usually heard and not seen—call in chorus during the wet months of spring. They are sometimes accompanied by wetland birds, including yellowthroats and red-winged blackbirds.

East of the wetlands, a scrubby, open woodland is inhabited by birds of drier, more protected habitats. The diminutive screech owl nests in tree hollows, and the rufous-sided eastern towhee, a black bird with rust and white sides and a pleasant call of *drink-your-tea* raises young in scratched depressions in the ground.

As might be expected from the types of vegetation in this area, flushing a ruffed grouse is a possibility. As the startled grouse dashes through the woods, the surprised observer can note the color phase of the individual bird—either red or gray, both of which occur in Lincoln. This is a beautifully feathered bird with mottled hues, and its varied diet is amply supplied by the collection of available plants: buds and catkins, from birch and aspen (poplar), as well as mountain ash berries, blueberries, and sheep laurel.

10
Wheeler Farm

General Information

The Wheeler Farm conservation land is a 54-acre property north of Lincoln Center. Within the preserved land, there are numerous signs of the land's past, among them a foundation and well, stone walls, orchard trees, and a range of ornamentals, some planted and some escaped. A stroll on the former farmland will not only reveal these evidences of the human hand, but also native trees, shrubs, and herbs and the various animals associated with them, which have slowly regained their hold on the property.

Parking

Limited parking is available on the shoulder of Wheeler Road by the trail entrance. One or two cars can also be parked along Lexington Road by the trail entrance near the pond northeast of the cemetery gates.

Links to Other Trails

The paths of the Wheeler conservation land connect with those of Flint's Pond and Flint Fields, and with those of the Cemetery.

History

Thomas Wheeler settled the property in 1717 and his descendants remained on the family land for nearly 250 years. The farm he established eventually specialized in fruit trees and dairy products. The Wheelers were thought of as bright intellectuals. Charles Stearns Wheeler (1817–1843), grandson of Dr. Charles Stearns, Lincoln's beloved pastor, was an active participant in the nineteenth-century Transcendentalist movement, whose adherents believed in the

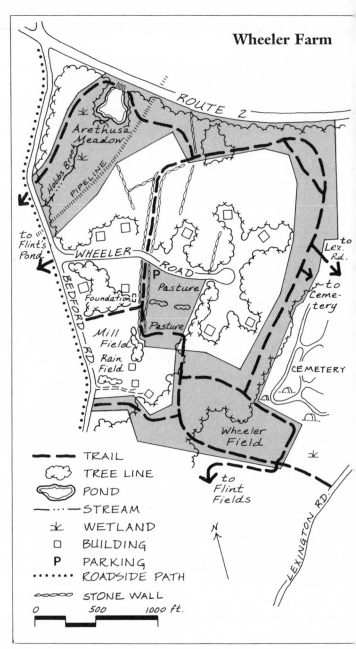

Wheeler Farm

ROUTE 2

Arethusa
Meadow

Hobbs Brook

PIPELINE

to
Flint's
Pond

WHEELER ROAD

BEDFORD RD.

P

Pasture

Pasture

Foundation

Mill
Field

Rain
Field

to
Lex.
Rd.

to
Cemetery

CEMETERY

Wheeler
Field

to
Flint
Fields

TRAIL
TREE LINE
POND
STREAM
WETLAND
BUILDING
P PARKING
ROADSIDE PATH
STONE WALL

0   500   1000 ft.

N

LEXINGTON RD.

divinity of human nature and that knowledge of reality is derived from intuitive sources rather than objective experience. Stearns Wheeler, as he was known, built himself a cabin on the shores of Flint's Pond, and here Thoreau visited him and got the idea for his experiment at Walden. Other family members were active in town politics, among them Stearns Wheeler's son of the same name, who served as town clerk and state legislator.

Preserved as a trail on the Wheeler property is a double-walled path used during Colonial times. The trail undoubtedly predated Bedford Road because the colonial homes face away from Bedford Road toward what was once the main thoroughfare, a farm road used, among other things, for leading cattle from one field to another.

Historical features along this colonial "road" include an old foundation and well, 375 feet southwest of Wheeler Road, and the remains of the Wheeler cider mill, located 200 feet beyond in an area called the Mill Field. The foundation of the mill, originally built as a carriage house, can be seen near a stand of non-native Douglas firs. Across the field is the overgrown Rain Field, so called because it seemed to rain every time the field was mowed. On the other side of Wheeler Road, as the trail approaches Route 2, there are old fruit trees, remains of the Wheeler orchard.

Acquisition

In 1965 the 109-acre Wheeler Farm was placed on the real-estate market. In order to preserve as much as possible of this valuable open space, the Lincoln Rural Land Foundation was established as a nonprofit conservation trust empowered to buy and sell land or to hold it for conservation purposes. Since that time, the Foundation has become a nationally recognized landmark of American conservation creativity.

The Foundation's initial financial backing was created by pledges of $10,000 from thirty Lincoln residents. With this borrowing power ensured, the organization purchased the Wheeler Farm, created a subdivision of eleven lots, and preserved 54 acres, which it transferred to the Lincoln Land Conservation Trust. This was the first time in the United States that a local nonprofit organization undertook this type of creative land conservation and development scheme, but today this approach is a standard practice called limited development.

Natural History

The main trail around the Wheeler Farm property follows an historic path flanked by stone walls, along a wooded hillside and an interesting rock ledge, past the Lexington Road Cemetery, and through a couple of pastures.

Suggested Walk: Trail loop from Wheeler Road

On Wheeler Road, 750 feet east of Bedford Road, the trail heads north down the slope and passes between the two old stone walls on either side of the trail. To the right, at the entrance to the wide trail, there are two dawn redwoods, and, as the trail leads north, large ash trees line the wall at intervals. The ashes are identified by evenly furrowed bark, blunt, thick twig ends, opposite branching, and compound leaves. Among the other vegetation are exotics such as burning bush and barberry, both common throughout the property, blackberries and other brambles, and some red cedars. At various places fresh signs of scraping and digging in the ground show that skunks that live in the stone walls have been looking for grubs.

At the first junction off this trail, take the trail to the left, heading northwest. This trail leads to a small pond adjacent to Route 2, before continuing on to Bedford Road and a connection to Flint's Pond. A prominent geological feature here is the river valley defined by the brook feeding this pond. This was the site of a glacial spillway from an-

cient Lake Sudbury during the last glacial period. By the pond, note the stone wall, most likely an old boundary marker. The wall is submerged, probably indicating that the pond was a shallow marsh before it was flooded by the construction of Route 2.

The Wheelers referred to the marsh as Arethusa Meadow for the spring-blooming orchid that once grew there. The showy two-inch-long flower, also called swamp pink, is named for Arethusa the fountain nymph, because it grows in bogs, wet meadows, and other watery habitats. Disturbances like the one caused at this particular site, as well as collecting, have caused this flower to become rare in the state. The pond is edged by red maple and highbush blueberry as well as some large white pines, some of them dead as a result of the rise in water level. A red-tailed hawk often perches in one of the pine snags and may nest in the large live pines nearby.

Return to the main trail, and take a left to continue on the trail loop that wanders through the woods. Many stone walls traverse the area, attesting to the once-cleared fields now covered with second-growth hardwoods, white pine, and hemlock. Covering the bumpy, rocky terrain are large patches of understory plants such as pipsissewa, pyrola, and bunchberry.

Eventually you will pass a rocky cliff on the right. Growing in the shady granite crevices is the evergreen wood fern, whose large bright fronds are most noticeable in the winter, when most of the surrounding vegetation is gray and brown. Continue on this trail, following the markers, with the swamp and Lexington Road Cemetery on your left.

A possible fall sighting in the adjacent lowland is the migrant winter wren, a chocolate-brown bird with an upturned tail that hunts for food among fallen tree trunks and overturned root clumps. As it looks for insects, it hops along the ground and flies only to reach protective cover. This wren's persistent call may even be heard when it passes through in autumn, despite the fact that nesting season is long over. Thoreau described its distinctive song in this way: "It reminded me of a fine corkscrew stream, issuing with incessant lisping tinkle from a cork, flowing rapidly, and I said that he had pulled out the spile and left it running."

As the trail heads out of the woods, running southwest, there is an excellent example of an esker, a snakelike ridge formed from deposits left as a stream ran beneath a melting glacier. At the field edge, the trail takes a sharp right and heads up the hill through a mixed woodland and a tangle of non-native shrubs and greenbriar. In autumn, the ground and rocks have pieces of hickory hulls on them, shucked by gray squirrels. As the squirrels prepare for winter, they bury and stow away nuts and acorns. High above, the squirrels' leafy nests are evident in crooks near the tree tops.

Continue to the top of the hill to the trail and take a sharp right that leads to the pasture gate. (A left at the trail leads back down the hill to Wheeler Field and Lexington Road.) It passes along a hedgerow of crabapples, honeysuckle, and multiflora rose near two houses. The trail back to Wheeler Road passes through a pasture of common field flowers such as yarrow, cinquefoil, and buttercups. Please take care to close the gate properly when you pass through.

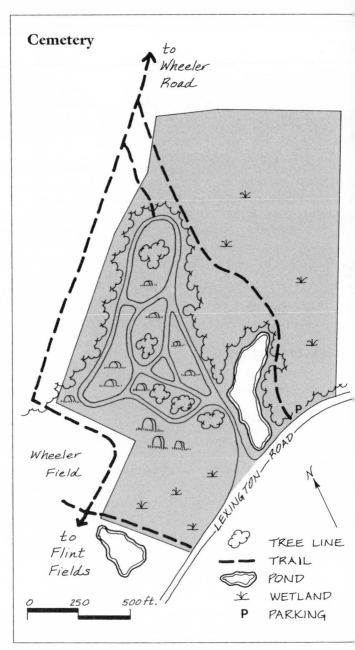

Cemetery

to Wheeler Road

to Wheeler Road

Wheeler Field

to Flint Fields

LEXINGTON—ROAD

P

N

0   250   500 ft.

🌳 TREE LINE

– – – TRAIL

⬭ POND

🌱 WETLAND

P   PARKING

76

11
Cemetery

General Information

This historic cemetery is surrounded on three sides by conservation land. In addition to the roadway that winds through the cemetery, passing beautiful ornamental and indigenous trees and lovely old headstones, trails on adjoining conservation land circle around the cemetery just beyond its border.

Parking

Parking for one or two cars is available along Lexington Road by the trail entrance near the pond northeast of the cemetery gates. Please note that the cemetery, and all conservation land, is open only from dawn to dusk.

Links to Other Trails

The cemetery trail connects with the Wheeler Farm conservation parcel and Flint Fields.

History and Acquisition

Buried within the town's three cemeteries are more than 250 years of Lincoln's heritage. The Lexington Road Cemetery contains the oldest burying ground, the one-acre Precinct Cemetery, received from Ephraim Flint in 1748. In recognition of his land donation, Ephraim was given a pew in the meetinghouse. The Precinct Cemetery has several fine examples of the colonial art of gravestone carving, for example, the winged face symbolizing the resurrection.

Thoreau visited the Precinct Cemetery in May of 1850. There he spoke with William F. Wheeler, who told him that five British soldiers, who died retreating from Concord on April 19, 1775, were buried there. Wheeler said that his grandfather, Edmund, had carried the fallen soldiers to their resting place in the cemetery. The Precinct Cemetery fell into disrepair when the Town Hill and Arbor Vitae Cemeteries were created. Subsequently, in 1884, George Bemis bought thirteen acres from the Flint family and donated it to the town for expansion of the original Precinct Cemetery. The enlarged cemetery, on a picturesque parcel chosen for its uneven terrain, was designed in the Natural Style, in keeping with the nineteenth-century Rural Cemetery Movement. William Wheeler, a civil engineer and landscape architect from Concord, laid out the winding roadways, which meander among undulating lawns and plantings of arboretum species such as flowering dogwood, mountain laurel, and rhododendron.

Additional acreage for the Cemetery was acquired from the Wheelers in 1927 and the developer of Oak Meadow, a nearby cluster development, in 1978. The statue of a boy and his dog at the cemetery entrance, donated by Mrs. James Storrow, was sculpted by Cyrus Dallin. An additional 7.3 acre parcel of conservation land adjacent to the Cemetery was donated in 1979 by Edward and Henry Flint in honor of their parents, Edward and Josephine Ritchie Flint.

Natural History

The pond that flanks the southeast side of the Cemetery was made in the early 1980s by James DeNormandie and Warren Flint, Sr. Pines and oaks reflect on the pond from the eastern side, and exotic plantings edge the pond here and there on the manicured western side. One alien horticultural variety originally planted there, Asiatic hydrangea, has now spread to the Flint swamp across Lexington Road; the escapees fill the wetland with white floral pompoms in midsummer. Birds that are attracted to the pond in summer include red-winged blackbirds and wood ducks.

Amphibians such as wood frogs and spring peepers

chorus loudly in early spring from the cemetery ponds and the vernal pool to the west of the entrance road. Large snapping turtles also make appearances in the area. The snapper generally weighs 10 to 35 pounds but can be as heavy as 85 pounds. Its characteristic features are a large head, a brown to black carapace, and a long tail with a saw-toothed edge along the upper side. Though known for its dangerous clamping jaw, this turtle is generally peaceful when underwater, pulling in its head when it is stepped on.

Plantings in cemeteries are well known for their attractiveness to birds. Though trees and shrubs are chosen principally for their beauty, many are amply endowed with fruits or foliage for cover and cavities for nesting. Norway spruces in a stately row, for example—evergreens of particular import for the winter beauty of the cemetery—serve as shelter, a place to nest, and a migratory stopover for a multitude of species. In cold weather, the dense branches harbor golden-crowned kinglets and chickadees; in summer, grackles, robins, and mourning doves nest in the spruce boughs; and, on a break during their May migration, black-throated green warblers look for insects near the treetops, enlivening the scene with flashes of sunny color and cheerful songs.

Wood pewees, small flycatchers that wait on the tips of

branches and sally into the open for airborne insects, were long common around the edge habitat of the cemetery. They would sing their clear plaintive *pee-a-wee* during warm summer evenings. Lately the wood pewee has become a rarer species, probably as a result of deforestation in its winter grounds. However, another musical songster, the wood thrush, can still be heard singing its flute-like song from the adjacent woodland during nesting season.

12
Flint Fields

General Information

Flint Fields are two adjoining agricultural fields, the South and North Field, totaling approximately 35 acres. Adjacent to Flint Fields, the hillside below Lincoln Hill has also been preserved, protecting a cherished part of the Lincoln landscape.

Parking

Limited parking is available at Bemis Hall on Bedford Road. One or two cars can be parked on the shoulder of Old Lexington Road by the trail entrance.

Links to Other Trails

The trail, which starts just below the curve of Old Lexington Road and runs through the woods along the top of the field, connects with the Wheeler property just across the stone wall bordering North Field, and runs from there to the Cemetery.

History

These fields are a portion of one of the oldest family farms in New England. They have been owned and farmed by the same family since the mid-seventeenth century. The land was part of a 750-acre grant deeded to Thomas Flint in the 1640s. Included in the tract was all of the land presently thought of as Lincoln town center and Flint's Pond, covering about 150 acres.

In the first decade of the eighteenth century, Flint's heir, Captain Ephraim Flint, became the first to farm the land. He built the farmhouse, which still stands near the end of the North Field, west of Lexington Road. Due to the

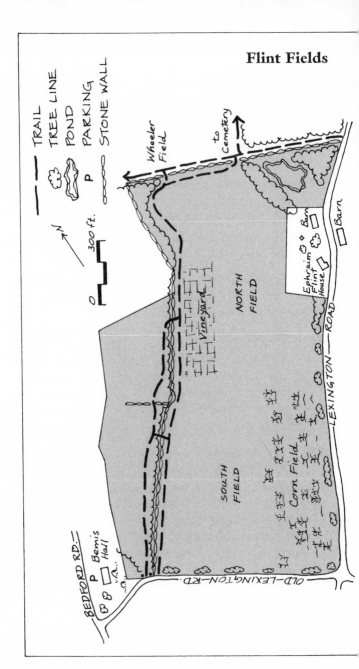

Flint Fields

TRAIL
TREE LINE
POND
P PARKING
STONE WALL

N
0 300 ft.

Wheeler Field

to Cemetery

Vineyard

NORTH FIELD

Ephraim Flint House

Barn

Barn

LEXINGTON ROAD

SOUTH FIELD

Corn Field

OLD LEXINGTON RD.

BEDFORD RD.
P
Bemis Hall

generosity of Edward and Henry Flint in 2004, this house is now protected from alteration by a historic preservation restriction.

Throughout the nineteenth century, the Boston market was supplied with produce from the Flint farm: fruits from the strawberry field and the apple orchard covering much of North Field and a wide variety of vegetables and pickling cucumbers. Hay fields and pasture land also supported a dairy herd. Then, in the early twentieth century, the Flints built four greenhouses in the North Field, extending the season and allowing for an expanded variety of market crops. Radishes, lettuce, cucumbers, tomatoes, and flowers were all grown there; unfortunately, the 1938 hurricane destroyed two of the greenhouses, and in the late 1940s another hurricane took the other two. Only a greenhouse chimney remains.

The old barn next to the Ephraim Flint house was moved from behind the white barn across the street to its present location in 1918. Recently, both the North and South fields have been used to grow silage corn and hay consisting of timothy, clover, and alfalfa. A portion of the North Field orchard, which had grown into a stand of ash trees, was cleared and a vineyard planted in 2003. The woodlands of Lincoln Hill have provided a natural backdrop to Flint Field for over a century. The successional hardwood forest has oak, hickory and white ash, with a lush undergrowth of poison ivy and alien invasive bittersweet.

Acquisition

A grand effort of grass-roots fund-raising and landowner generosity culminated in 1989, with the successful preservation of Flint Fields, a unique agricultural and historic treasure. Participants included the Flint family, the Lincoln Conservation Commission and other town boards, the Lincoln Land Conservation Trust, abutters, and many committed town residents. The Warren Flint, Sr. family sold development rights on the South Field to the Town for less than half the market value of the land. The permanent restriction on the field continued agricultural use while prohibiting development and other activities inconsistent with the land's natural, scenic, and open character. The North Field was sold to the town outright under very favorable terms by Henry and Edward Flint. It is now under cultivation and permanent conservation use. In 2004, Edward and Henry Flint donated an historic preservation restriction on their historic home to ensure that the interior and exterior of this colonial home continues to match the protected colonial landscape.

In 2004 the Rural Land Foundation acquired the rights to a 17-acre house and lot adjacent to the fields from the Stanley Heck estate. Over a four-month period, with the assistance of the Lincoln Land Conservation Trust, Community Preservation Committee, and donations of many citizens, the Rural Land Foundation protected approximately eight acres including the wooded hillside above the South Field, as well as a strip along Bedford Road.

Conserving these parcels has been essential to retaining the rural character of the historic center of Lincoln. Together, these parcels are a testament to the importance of preserving agricultural land and to the careful stewardship of one family for three and a half centuries.

Natural History

As the seasons progress, these fertile fields are frequented by songbirds, migrating geese, waterfowl, and even some shorebirds. Among the shorebirds is the killdeer, an early spring arrival. This plover, white on the breast with two dark neck rings, chooses areas near open fields and gardens to nest. At least one pair has nested each year somewhere behind Henry Flint's house. As haying progresses in July,

coyote pups

young killdeers accompany their parents onto the fields, making the most of insects that the mowing has revealed. Despite the independence of the young, the parents keep close watch, playing a broken-wing trick as a distraction when anything threatening approaches.

Indigo buntings are often seen around the field edges, singing from May into early summer, while wood thrushes voice their sweet refrain from the woods at the top of the fields. Flocks of robins that arrive in the spring probe for worms in the upper part of the South Field. Meadowlarks and bobolinks were former summer residents but have not been observed for many years.

Swallows also follow the haying equipment, foraging over the field for insects exposed by the cutting. Fair numbers of barn and tree swallows gather—sometimes scores of them filling the air. As fall approaches, migrants begin to come through. A solitary sandpiper may appear at the small pond behind the Ephraim Flint house, and blackbirds and grackles often congregate in the fields and the nearby row of ash trees along the stone wall that edges the Wheeler property.

Later in fall, dull-colored pipits may be seen camouflaged against the tilled field and, during the winter, bluebirds and robins provide a splash of color and snow buntings infrequently dot the snow-covered meadow. The lovely buntings, residents of more northern climes, grace us with their presence only during the most severe winters when they are forced southward due to heavy snows that cover the weed and grass seeds on which they feed.

As frequently occurs along field edges, the wall bordering the Wheeler Field is overgrown with alien invasive species such as barberry, bittersweet, and winged euonymus, as well as poison ivy. Nearby is an overgrown orchard, with several kinds of fruit trees. On the tree trunks, yellow-bellied sapsuckers have left their patterns of impressions, little rows of horizontal drill holes from which the birds drink the sap with their uniquely adapted brush-like tongues. The tiny holes may also be visited by other animals such as chipmunks, squirrels, and even butterflies, which share a fancy for the sweet sap. Pileated woodpeckers, rarely seen but often heard, frequent the woods of Lincoln Hill.

Predatory birds appear regularly at Flint Fields and other portions of the farm at almost any time of year. Resident red-tailed hawks like the big oak at the top of South Field. If not mobbed by crows, they have a comfortable view of the wide terrain where small mammals can be found. In mild winters, kestrels overwinter and hunt near farm buildings for mice and an occasional small songbird.

Canada geese, the resident population long separate from their migrating cousins, graze in these fields all year long in flocks of up to 600 birds for several hours, usually in the morning and late afternoon. Coyotes, which are known to hunt Canada geese as well as field rodents, are seen by the fields. A sighting is most likely at dawn or dusk.

At 25 inches at the shoulder on average, the grizzly-gray coyotes are often mistaken for large dogs, but distinguishing features are their pale eyes, long legs and long bushy tails.

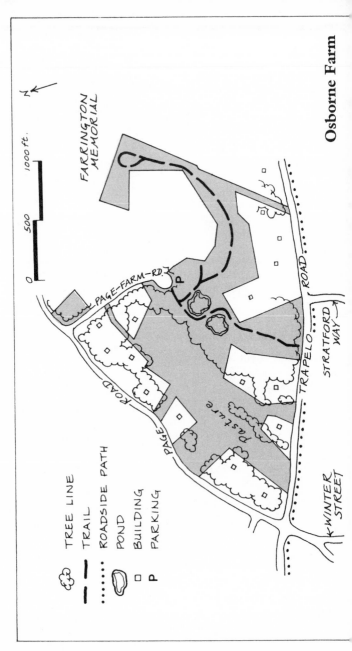

Osborne Farm

13
Osborne Farm

General Information

The Osborne Farm parcel off Page Road consists of 17 acres of pasture south of Page Farm Road and 24 acres of wooded land to the east. Several acres of Howland land on the west side of Page Road south of the barn have also been protected. All this property was an important part of a farm owned by Gordon and Marjorie Osborne.

Parking

Limited parking is available on the shoulder of Page Farm Road in the cul-de-sac near the trail entrance. Parking is not allowed on Trapelo or Page Roads.

Links to Other Trails

The Trapelo Road bike path provides a link to Silver Hill Road, the Cannon-Holden Fields, and Silver Hill Bog. Efforts continue to create links to the Cemetery and Flint Fields by heading west across the Flint esker.

History

This land has been continuously occupied since before 1750. The Page Farm House, which still stands on the property, was substantially expanded by Boston attorney and sea captain S.B. Thompson in the 1850s when the new Lincoln railroad encouraged development of summer homes in town. The house also had been a stop on the Underground Railway. Farmed sporadically over much of its earlier history, in the 1950s and 1960s Gordon Osborne raised Black Angus beef cattle and used sheep on the lawn to trim the grass. Osborne piped music down to the two ponds and people from all over Lincoln enjoyed evening skating parties there. Many of the trails, fences, and stone bridge are part of the original carriage paths. The carriage path between the two ponds that entered from Trapelo Road was the formal entrance, while most access was from the easier "back door" route off Page Road. In recent years, the northern and larger pond was deepened and the stone bridge repaired as a neighborhood project to preserve the landscape.

Acquisition

This property, protected largely through three efforts between the 1970s and 2004, illustrates the variety of techniques used in the town's conservation transactions. The first effort involved a private family that generously donated both a permanent and a term-based conservation restriction on a portion of their land while retaining ownership. Second, a private developer used the town's cluster zoning by-law, augmented by a generous initiative by neighbors, to protect additional land. Most recently, the Rural Land Foundation used both its customary conservation subdivision techniques and private donations to complete permanent protection of the majority of the original Osborne Farm, with the land now owned by the Lincoln Land Conservation Trust and protected by a conservation restriction to the Town of Lincoln.

Natural History

The Osborne Farm land shows the evidence of the many years of human habitation in its fields, fences, carriage paths, and bridge over the ponds. But these "improvements" have a settled look and remind the visitor of how much has been left undisturbed. The fields are populated by a small herd of Red Devon cattle, a rare breed being preserved largely through small farms. A coyote and a large flock of turkeys regularly visit the fields and a family of foxes lives nearby.

The two ponds are home to a muskrat and black racer and northern water snakes. The snakes sun on the warm rocks and drape themselves in blueberry bushes and on fallen trees by the smaller pond, sometimes startling the unwary visitor. Belted kingfishers fly overhead, giving their rattling call. Great blue herons stalk fish and mallards nest in the larger pond.

In the stand of hemlock beyond the ponds, one often sees a flash of white as a white-tailed deer flicks its tail and runs off. Still deeper in the woods in early spring, skunk cabbage, lady's slippers, and wild geraniums flourish, along with the "quacking" vocalizations of wood frogs in nearby vernal pools. Under the stand of white pine trees watch for owls; barred and great horned owls nest nearby. Partridge-berry with its small deep-green leaves and bright red berries mats this area year round.

Suggested walk: A Loop Trail from Page Farm Road or Trapelo Road

Trail access is from the end of the Page Farm Road cul de sac. As you walk in, you will pass the fields on your right.

Following the trail over the recently restored stone bridge, you will pass on your right houses along Trapelo

Road and will cross two intermittent streams that flow into the swampy area on the left. These straight streams were probably dug by farmers in an era when the impacts of altering the landscape were less well understood. As you head deeper into the woods, you will eventually loop back through a stand of white pines abutting the 80-acre Farrington Memorial property, which is used for the benefit of needy children.

To enter from Trapelo Road, hike in on the marked trail that starts to the east of the Page Farm fields and nearby driveway. As you walk in through the woods, you will come shortly to the restored stone bridge.

14
Pierce Park

General Information

Pierce Park is located in the center of Lincoln at the corner of Weston and Lincoln Roads. It consists of 30 acres of land including a large house, lawns, two ponds, and woods behind the house. The park is a popular spot for picnics and related activities, and the Pierce House is used for both public and private functions.

Behind the Town Offices are playing fields that can be used with permission from the Lincoln Recreation Department. The Smith-Andover field, a small open meadow of four acres that lies northwest of Lincoln Road across from the Town Offices, provides a connecting path to Sandy Pond Road. The field is dotted with young black walnut trees, and a triangular bench at the highest point makes a pleasant place to sit and reflect.

Parking

Parking is available in the lot behind Pierce House (except during Pierce House functions) and at the Town Offices. There is no parking allowed on Lincoln or Weston Roads or along the Pierce House driveway.

Links to Other Trails

The trail which crosses the meadow south of the Pierce House emerges on Weston Road and connects with the trail crossing the Donaldson Field. A trail to the southwest ends on a driveway just before Beaver Pond Road, across which is the Peirce Hill Trail.

History

The Pierce Park land was part of the Flint grant in the mid-1600s. It was first sold to the Bond family, then the Meade

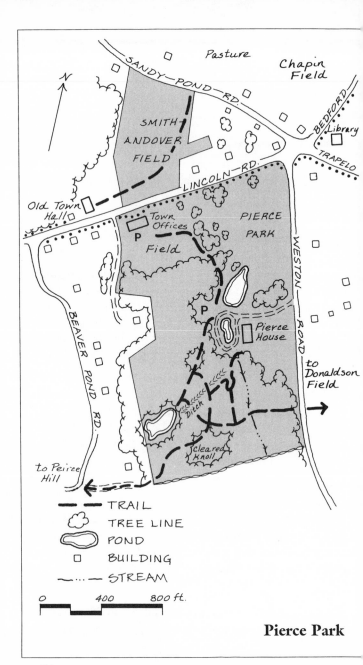

TRAIL

TREE LINE

POND

BUILDING

STREAM

0   400   800 ft.

Pierce Park

family, and finally to Samuel Hoar in 1810. Samuel Hoar's son changed his name from Abijah Pierce Hoar to Abijah Hoar Pierce, which became the family name for future generations. His son, John Howard Pierce, was the builder, in 1900, of the Pierce House, a classic American Georgian residence. The architectural design of the front facade of the main part of the house is based upon that of the Vassal-Craigie-Longfellow House, built in 1759, on Brattle Street in Cambridge.

John Pierce landscaped the estate grounds with lawns and rows of trees in keeping with the formal architecture; records from 1931 show that a pine grove and some hemlocks, still standing between the Pierce House and the Town Offices, were planted on the property. Rows of maples and elms were planted along Weston Road and the eastern and southern boundaries of the property; red and white pine were placed in a line by the driveway; and lombardy poplars were arranged in a double row along the brook. About 1900, Lincoln Road was realigned, and the wall along the road was raised. Today, an observant passerby may see the old and new parts of the wall. A pamphlet entitled "A Tree Identification Trail" focuses on the trees on the grounds of Pierce Park and the Lincoln Public Library. This pamphlet, published in 2004, is available at the Library or the Town Offices.

Acquisition

In his will written in 1907, John Pierce stated that upon the death of his daughter Elsie, he bequeathed his farm and house in Lincoln to the inhabitants of Lincoln to be used as a hospital and park. At Town Meeting in 1927, residents voted to accept the gift, provided that the wills were modified so that the town did not have to use the property for a hospital. It was also agreed that Elsie's brother would be granted use of the house and property for the remainder of his life. In 1964 the town finally acquired the estate.

Natural History

The open portions of Pierce Park were used for hay until
the mid-1940s, when the town began to maintain it as a
recreational area. The ponds, created to help drain the
open lawn and serve as skating ponds, were dug in 1965.
The larger pond near the house, popular for skating in
winter, is also a favorite place for "ponding" to find various invertebrates, frogs, and fish.

Schoolchildren visit the pond annually to collect pond
life, which they observe carefully and then release. Frogs
are always a highlight for the students, but unfortunately
all species have been diminishing in numbers in recent decades. The bullfrogs call *jug-a-rum* on a June afternoon,
and the green frogs make a banjolike *plunk* as they jump
from the bank into the water.

The students have also discovered many small, interesting invertebrates in the pond, some that live on the muddy
bottom and others that float on the surface film or swim
around just beneath it. Many-legged crustaceans such as
scuds and isopods scavenge for food near the pond bottom. The various freshwater snails feed on algae and other
plants, and the diving beetles capture and consume insects
and small water animals. On the water surface, it is easy to

find insects, such as water striders, which skate on the surface of the water on delicate legs.

The pond is a breeding ground for frogs and flying insects. The tadpoles of bullfrogs, especially the third-year ones, are giants. Mosquito larvae hang from the surface with siphons above the water providing them with air, and the large-mouthed bulgy-eyed dragonfly nymphs, not at all like their lovely parents, cruise the muddy bottom until ready to metamorphose into a winged adult.

Canada geese are regular spring inhabitants of the pond and from time to time, a mallard, green heron, or great blue heron arrives. The great blue, feathered in bluish grey, has long, slender legs and a long, sharp beak for fishing; it wades patiently among the cattails, quietly stalking its prey. Much of the time it waits and watches; then it strikes and pulls up a crayfish or catfish from the water.

Two short trails, lined in one section by a large dewberry patch, lead from the driveway and parking area through a mix of pine, white birch, red oak, and red maples to a pond

and a grassy knoll dotted with low-growing field junipers and red cedars. In the woods, there are some old wolf pines and some open-growth oaks, their many giant limbs low to the ground. These giant, spreading trees give a hint that the area was once open. An unusual walled ditch connects the pond in the woods to the stream which flows by Pierce House. Other trails lead from the grassy knoll to Weston Road and to Beaver Pond Road.

15
Lincoln Fields

General Information

The three parcels that make up Lincoln Fields represent one of the Town's most recent large-scale preservation initiatives, resulting in 38 acres of permanent open space, including 28 acres of open agricultural fields; creation of over a mile of public trails; preservation of widely enjoyed vistas; protection of land important to wildlife; and protection of the historic character of the Town Center.

Parking

For the Cannon-Holden Field, limited parking is available by the riding ring at the north end of Browning Fields on Weston Road. For the Donaldson and Chapin Fields, parking is available in the lot behind Pierce House, except during Pierce House functions, and at the Town Offices. There is no parking allowed on Sandy Pond Road, Weston Road or along the Pierce House driveway.

Acquisition

The Lincoln Fields Project was spearheaded by Lincoln's three conservation organizations: the Rural Land Foundation, the Lincoln Land Conservation Trust, and the Conservation Commission. Inspired by the generosity of all the owners of the parcels in offering the land at well below market value, the three organizations pledged 25 percent of the total cost, and successfully raised the rest from private donations.

Natural History

The open fields on these three parcels provide valuable foraging habitat for birds and mammals. It is particularly im-

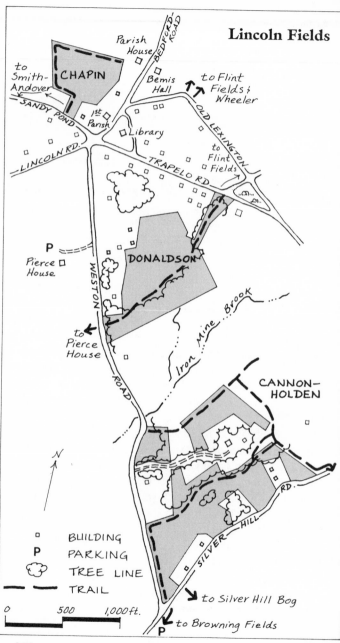

Lincoln Fields

Parish House

BEDFORD ROAD

to Smith-Andover

CHAPIN

Bemis Hall

to Flint Fields & Wheeler

SANDY POND

1st Parish

Library

OLD LEXINGTON

to Flint Fields

LINCOLN RD.

TRAPELO RD.

P

Pierce House

DONALDSON

WESTON

to Pierce House

Iron Mine Brook

ROAD

CANNON-HOLDEN

N

SILVER HILL RD.

□ BUILDING

P PARKING

🌳 TREE LINE

▬ ▬ TRAIL

0   500   1,000 ft.

to Silver Hill Bog

to Browning Fields

P

portant for small mammals, such as mice, voles and moles. Deer, fox, coyote, mink, weasels, and other large mammals needing significant open land are regularly seen in the fields, as are birds of prey. The shrubs along the field edges provide excellent nesting habitat for songbirds, including the American robin, gray catbird, common yellowthroat and blue-winged warbler.

Chapin Field

The Chapin Field is located behind the First Parish Church and Parish House, with frontage on Sandy Pond Road. The five-and-a-half-acre open field has been in agricultural use for over two hundred years. When the field was purchased by the Chapins in the 1830's, it was used for fruit crops, such as strawberries, apples and peaches. Several old orchard trees still remain. It is currently hayed.

Cannon-Holden Fields

The Cannon-Holden Fields are located at the corner of Weston and Silver Hill Roads. The property contains over twelve acres of open fields, with the remaining six acres of developed land in rolling wooded hillside. Trails on the property provide links to Browning Field North and to the Silver Hill bog. The land also preserves an important wildlife corridor along Iron Mine Brook. The large field at the corner has been in agricultural use for well over 150 years. In the early 1900's, there were greenhouses, where flowers and fruit crops were raised. The field is currently hayed by Codman Community Farms.

Donaldson Field

The 15-acre Donaldson Field is located across from Pierce Park between Weston and Trapelo Roads. The trail along the eastern edge of the field connects Pierce Park with the bike path on Trapelo Road. The parcel encompasses ten acres of open field and five acres of adjoining wetlands and woodlands. The Donaldson Field has been in agricultural production since the 1700s, and was in the Donaldson family for nearly 100 years. Earlier in this century, the field was used as an orchard and for the pasturage of farm animals. Recently, it has been hayed by Codman Community Farms.

16
Silver Hill Bog/ Chapman Pasture

General Information

The 26 acres of bog, swamp, open water, woods, and pasture and the flora and fauna of these habitats make this property a wonderful place for those interested in botany or bird watching. Trails in the woods are open and accessible, with boardwalks placed over swampy areas to provide access during all but the wettest times of year. Horses are discouraged, and prohibited during wet conditions. Trails through the bogs are on sphagnum moss growing over or around tree roots, and the footing is often irregular and unsupported. Boots should be worn in these sections. Trails across the pasture are no longer discernible but persons may walk directly across the land and through gates at several locations in the fence. Walkers must be sure to close all gates behind them, and dogs are not permitted in the pasture even if leashed.

Parking

Limited parking is available by the pond just north of the trail entrance on Silver Hill Road. A few spaces also exist by the riding ring at the north end of Browning Field on Weston Road.

Links to Other Trails

From the Silver Hill and Chapman Pasture trails, there are connections to the Cannon-Holden Fields, Pigeon Hill and Browning Fields, and thence to Beaver Pond.

History

Since the area was first colonized, there have been many farms on this section of land. The northern portion was

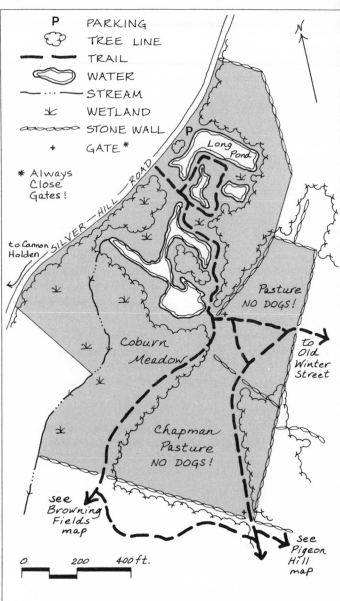

P   PARKING

TREE LINE

TRAIL

WATER

·—···— STREAM

WETLAND

STONE WALL

+   GATE *

* Always
Close
Gates!

to Cannon
Holden

SILVER—HILL—ROAD

P

Long Pond

Pasture
NO DOGS!

to
Old
Winter
Street

Coburn
Meadow

Chapman
Pasture
NO DOGS!

see
Browning
Fields
map

see
Pigeon
Hill
map

0   200   400 ft.

Silver Hill Bog/Chapman Pasture

once part of the Benjamin Monroe farm and the southern section was farmland belonging to Benjamin Brown. Formerly named Eighteen-Acre Meadow, the Silver Hill Bog area provided hay for the farm animals, and the Chapman Pasture and other upland areas were used as grazing land for cattle in the nineteenth and twentieth centuries.

In the early 1900s, the bog bordering Silver Hill Road was valued for its peat formed by decomposed sphagnum moss. When this was removed from the wetland, an open body of water was created, measuring roughly 70 feet by 240 feet. Now known as Long Pond, it was once used for cutting ice. Similarly created smaller ponds exist elsewhere in the parcel.

Acquisition

The Silver Hill Bog area parcels were given to the Lincoln Land Conservation Trust as one of its first acquisitions, and Coburn Meadow was acquired later. The permanent protection of Chapman Pasture, accomplished in 1964, is an example of what neighbors and concerned parties can accomplish quickly, without having to wait for town meeting action. The land would certainly have been lost to development if abutters and friends had not been able to act through the Lincoln Land Conservation Trust, each making a contribution to the Trust, which promptly purchased the entire pasture.

Natural History

A short loop trail, including a boardwalk across flooded sections, provides unusual access to a bog habitat. The bog was formed in a kettlehole. Ice left by the retreating glacier melted and created a pond whose water level fluctuates and which is fed by slow-moving tributaries. Located near the head of a small valley, the pond collects water from the north and east. The outflow heads south toward Browning Fields, eventually joining Stony Brook.

A bog is characterized by a thick carpet of sphagnum moss and many distinctive species. Decomposition in a bog is severely hindered by the highly acidic environment, and as sphagnum moss and other plants grow, they compress the previous plant growth with their weight to form dense mats of floating vegetation. The acidic nature of bogs not only limits the variety of plant life that can live in it, but also allows unique species to prosper, many of which are not found in other wetland habitats. The Silver Hill Bog supports both traditional bog plants and those more common in emergent marshes. Unfortunately, invasive buckthorn, combined with natural succession (including poison sumac), is rapidly changing the bog vegetation.

Suggested Walk: a loop from Silver Hill Bog to Chapman Pasture and south, returning on Silver Hill Road.

About 30 yards in from Silver Hill Road, the Long Pond Trail loop splits off to the left, circles to the right around a small bog, passes the southwestern edge of Long Pond, and continues on to rejoin the main trail. Long Pond itself, now partially obscured from the trail by buckthorn, is mostly filled marshland, with a large stand of cattails growing in the standing water which remains in its center. Look for skunk cabbage, especially in the early spring when the mottled purple spathe pushes up. Black chokeberry is common along here, with its white flowers in early spring resembling those of the apple, its cousin. Other shrubs include highbush blueberry, swamp azalea, alder, winterberry, and poison sumac (be careful what you touch!). Glossy buckthorn, an invasive plant, is abundant. It can be identified by its tiny, clustered, greenish flowers and speckled branches.

In the main part of the bog, the ubiquitous light-green moss is sphagnum, which constitutes the base of vegetation of the mat, and beside the boardwalk is the small, fragile round-leaved sundew. Only a few inches tall and hidden in the sphagnum, this miniature plant snares insects. The delicate, dew-tipped red hairs on the leaves trap small insects, then the leaves close around them.

At the edge of the water, several typical bog species can be seen. Leatherleaf is common, the intertwined woody roots strengthening the sphagnum mat, and large cranberry, a low-growing vine and relative of the blueberry, lies almost in the water.

Pitcher plants grow among the sphagnum; it is easiest to see them in the winter and early spring when their hollow red tubes stand out against the light green sphagnum. Like the sundews, pitcher plants trap insects, utilizing them as a source of nitrogen.

Mammals that prosper in this area include rabbits, mice, foxes, skunks, and opossums. A variety of songbirds are common, including red-winged blackbirds, common yellowthroats, Carolina wrens, and catbirds. Both the catbird and Carolina wren prefer tangles and thickets like those bordering the bog. The catbirds feed on the abundant berries, and the wrens find spiders and insects of the wetland habitat. The feline mewing of the catbirds is unmistakable, as is the loud, clear voice of the Carolina wren.

After the ice melts in the spring, the shallow pools fill with algae and, following spring rains, several frog species begin calling: spring peepers and wood frogs in late March or April, pickerel frogs in the middle of April, green frogs and American toads in May, and the larger gray tree frogs by June. Wood frogs and spotted salamanders migrate to the same vernal pools each spring from their woodland

homes to lay eggs. On the first mild rainy night in March or April, this migration occurs and Silver Hill Road is closed to traffic to prevent mortality as the amphibians cross the road.

Numerous invertebrate species also inhabit the bog. Tiny crustaceans—cyclops, water fleas, ostracods, isopods, and amphipods—harvest the algae at almost a microscopic level, and these in turn provide food for a variety of water insects such as water striders, backswimmers, water boatmen, whirligig and diving beetles, and the flies: stoneflies, mayflies, dragonflies, damselflies, and caddisflies.

Leaving the bog loop, bear left on the trail in a southeasterly direction. The path is covered with partridgeberry and thick mats of moss until the trail becomes drier and white pines become the predominant tree, forming columns as a foreground for the Chapman Pasture beyond. After a short distance, there is a gate on the left of the trail which is an entrance to Chapman Pasture. Walkers can cross Chapman Pasture heading east to connect with Old Winter Street or south to join Pigeon Hill trails. Because Chapman Pasture contains sheep, do not bring dogs into it and please be sure to close all gates behind you. Dogs and their companions are asked to continue on the main trail which continues on in a southwesterly direction through the woodlands that border the pasture.

The open pasture is frequented by numerous birds. The gnarled and knotty branches of the fruit trees provide nesting cover for robins and cavities for house wrens, house finches, bluebirds, and other cavity-nesting birds. Bluebird houses have also successfully attracted residents. Also active in the field in summer are cardinals, probably nesting nearby as well, and killdeers, which noisily scold the sheep. Joining the others in flight over the pasture are the graceful barn swallows; they sweep the grassy hillside with open beaks, catching insects on the wing, then return to feed their young waiting in barnyard nests lined with feathers and cemented with mud to overhead beams.

If you do not enter Chapman Pasture but continue on the main trail with the pasture on your left, you will be in primarily deciduous woodland, which is often very wet underfoot in the spring. These woods were once cleared, hence the name "Coburn Meadow." A small area of open

water and some lily pads can be found on the right hand side of the trail and various species of frogs call from the swamp.

Further along at a fork in the trail, the path to the left up the hill leads to the Pigeon Hill trails. Note a large patch of jack-in-the-pulpit near this intersection. The main trail continues on, passing behind a private home. As the trail crosses a little stream, look for tracks in the muddy bank or creek bed—perhaps some deer tracks or maybe a raccoon's paw prints. When the trail opens into a field, bear left out to a long driveway with a well-maintained cattle pasture beyond. Turn right down the driveway to return to Silver Hill Road. The distance along Silver Hill Road between the driveway entrance and the trail entrance at Long Pond is approximately one-quarter mile. Alternatively, one may cross Silver Hill Road and join the Cannon-Holden trails around the field, looping back to Silver Hill Road opposite the entrance to the bog.

17

Browning Fields/ Pigeon Hill

General Information

This conservation land includes three areas, connected by trails, some of them through private land. The 65 acres of land support a variety of wildlife and include a varied terrain of field, swamp, and woodland, as well as well-marked, well-maintained trails and boardwalks. Horseback riding is permitted on trails through drier sections of the property.

Parking

Parking for a few cars is available by the riding ring at the north end of Browning Field North on Weston Road.

Links to Other Trails

From Browning Field North there are connections to Pigeon Hill, the Cannon-Holden Fields, Silver Hill Bog and Chapman Pasture. From Browning South a trail connects across Weston Road to the Beaver Pond trails.

History

Benjamin Brown was a prominent early-1700s landowner in this part of Lincoln (then West Watertown) who acquired approximately 500 acres of land during his lifetime, mostly east of Weston Road. Born in Watertown in 1687, Brown settled in West Watertown in a house still standing on Conant Road. Included in his holdings were this land as well as Silver Hill Bog and swampland north of Pigeon Hill, known then as the Remote Pine Meadow.

   Benjamin left most of the land to his sons, Benjamin Jr., Timothy, and Joseph. Timothy inherited Browning Fields

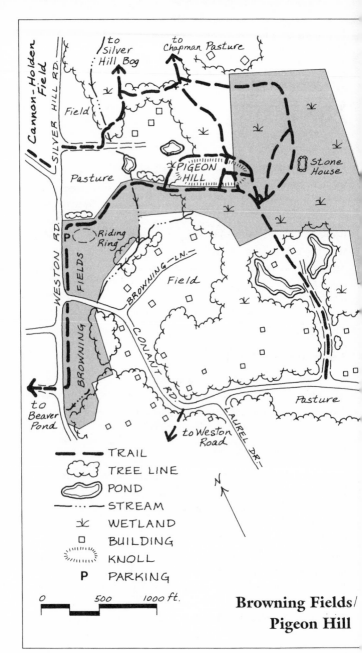

to Silver Hill Bog

to Chapman Pasture

Cannon-Holden Field

SILVER HILL RD.

Field

WESTON RD.

Pasture

PIGEON HILL

Stone House

P Riding Ring

FIELDS

BROWNING LN.

Field

BROWNING

CONANT RD.

to Beaver Pond

to Weston Road

LAUREL DR.

Pasture

- - - TRAIL
TREE LINE
POND
···· STREAM
WETLAND
□ BUILDING
KNOLL
P PARKING

N

0   500   1000 ft.

**Browning Fields/
Pigeon Hill**

and the land to the top of Pigeon Hill on the east and north as well as Benjamin Brown's house; Joseph settled on the land to the east of Timothy's. Deacon Benjamin Brown and his heirs continued to farm until 1881. The farms were made up of orchards, swampland for hay production, pasture, and a woodlot.

Acquisition

The effort to save Browning Fields and Pigeon Hill began in 1960 and continued for over two decades. The long process involved hours of meetings and complex negotiations between the owners, neighbors, the Lincoln Conservation Commission, and the Lincoln Land Conservation Trust, as well as matching funds for acquisition from the both the state and federal governments. In the end, the hard work paid off, and a wonderful series of contiguous parcels were preserved that otherwise would have been lost to development.

Natural History

These two fields have been farmed for centuries—the southern one as a hayfield for over 50 years and the northern one as cropland and a hayfield. Look for a variety of birds in the fields, including bluebirds, killdeers, red-tailed hawks, red-winged blackbirds, and swallows.

In 1991, for the first time in several years, bobolinks nested in the fields. The location is favored by the bobolinks because of the grassy meadow and the stream running along the border. In late spring, the male bubbles with song from the air, from trees, from the ground. By June, the pair builds its nest in a thick tussock, concealing it with entwined grasses and lining it with soft material. When the young hatch, the parents feed them grasshoppers, crickets, and other insects that are abundant in the field until, by mid-July, the offspring are able to fend for themselves. By arrangement with Codman Community Farms, which mows the fields, the first cut of hay is not taken until mid-July on Browning Field North in order that the young bobolinks may fledge safely.

Another songbird, the feisty gray eastern kingbird, also likes this spot for flycatching in the field. The male is tyrannical—as his Latin name, *Tyrannidae*, indicates. He exposes the brightly contrasting red-orange patch on his head in display when necessary and aggressively defends the nest from all intruders no matter how large; hawks and crows are favored targets.

Both red-tailed hawks and red-shouldered hawks may perch on oak branches at the field edge and circle the sky, soaring with classic buteo silhouettes. Red-shouldered hawks have nested in the woods south of Conant Road for many years.

Woodcocks, which used to nest in Browning Fields, are most active at dusk and are known for their habit of prob-

ing for worms and grubs in the earth. As early as mid-
March, listen for their whistling wings and their *peent*
courtship call. The nighthawk, another bird most common
at dusk, passes through during migration in August, when
hundreds may fly and wheel overhead. Because of the vast
open expanse of sky, Browning Fields is a good place to
watch for them.

Small invertebrates are abundant in Browning Field, especially in summer. Look for little mounds of froth on
grass stems; inside are the eggs or the little green nymph
of the harmless spittle bug. On warm evenings, fireflies are
numerous over the field, signaling to each other. Spiders
are also busy at night spinning and repairing their webs.
These webs are a gorgeous sight on a dewy morning when
the sun is shining on them.

*Suggested Walk: Browning Field North to the stone house
and back*

Follow the trail that skirts along the northern edge of the
field bordering the adjacent cattle pasture. The stream,
which you will cross, runs south through Browning Fields;
it meanders through cattails and past a row of weeping willows and red osier dogwood before going under Conant
Road and underground in the lower (south) field.

Along the stream and in the back part of the field, flourish goldenrod, Queen Anne's lace, spotted Joe Pye weed,
Canada lily, devil's paint brush, black-eyed Susan, blue
flag, and milkweed, the silky milkweed seeds floating in the
breeze on a cool fall day. The invasive purple loosestrife is
starting to appear; in 2003, beetles from the genus *Galeru-
cella* were released to try to control the spread of the
loosestrife by biological means. Look for sensitive and
royal fern growing along the path as it heads toward the
woods from the riding ring—and beware of seasonally
abundant poison ivy! Common yellowthroat warblers nest
regularly in this area near the stream.

On entering the hushed woods, one finds oneself in a stand of white pines, surrounded by several species of ferns, including hay-scented and cinnamon. The large trees are descendants of the few that remained after the hurricane of 1938. Head left along the barbed wire fence. The marked trail soon takes a right and crosses a small stony brook to a stone wall. Upon crossing the brook on a duckboard, you will notice some flame and plumb azalea, shrubs planted by Paul Brooks in the 1960s. Now bear left and ascend a gently sloping hill. This small knoll in the middle of the woods, with the stone wall running north-south over it, is called Pigeon Hill because flocks of the now-extinct passenger pigeon once gathered there in the great oaks.

Club moss and ground pine are bright, even in the brown of winter, and winter birds also add cheer in the snowy woods: chickadees, white-breasted nuthatches and an occasional red-breasted nuthatch (formerly the more common of the two species), cardinals, white-throated sparrows, juncos, tufted titmice, and golden-crowned kinglets.

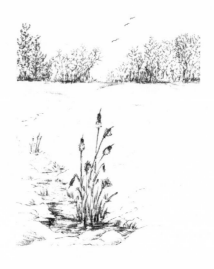

In spring, forest wildflowers and herbs are a lovely feature of Pigeon Hill and its woodlands. The most notable of them are starflower, pink lady's slipper, blue violet, Solomon's seal, and Jack-in-the-pulpit. In addition, escaped periwinkle, with its blue five-petaled flowers, is a pretty ground cover in the woodland.

The trail continues down the north side of the hill, and a boardwalk leads through the wooded swamp. In spring, the swamp rings with the sounds of wood frogs and spring peepers and is verdant with luxuriant jewelweed, skunk cabbage, and yellow iris shoots.

Over a century ago, the swampland was used for harvesting hay and blueberries and also for cranberry production. In addition to swamp azalea, red maple and alder, white pines are becoming established, representing a later stage in the succession from wet meadow to wooded swamp. Red maples are easily identified in the middle of April by the red flowers that precede the leaves, and in early fall when the leaves turn brilliant red. Unusual flora seen in the swamp include a white cardinal flower, closed bottle gentian, wild yellow flax, and fringed gentian. After a small rise, the trail takes a right toward the sheep pasture. Approaching the pasture gate, a left fork leads up the hill (paralleling the stone wall) and down to join the trail to the Silver Hill Bog. The right fork, after crossing a wet area on planks, follows a stone wall on the north, makes a slight rise as it turns south and descends to cross a small stream on duckboards. At the next fork, bear left. A gentle slope leads to the ruins of an old stone house. These ruins are all that remain of a cabin built by Merrill Hunt and his son in the 1920s, hauling all of the materials by sled from their home on Conant Road. The dwelling, with its beautiful stonework and perfect archway, was nearly finished when the hardship of the Great Depression put an end to this ambitious family project.

The trail leading south downhill from the stone house

passes through the pine woods. Beneath the white pines near the trail junction southwest of the stone house, look for great-horned owl pellets on the pine needles. These gray sausage-shaped bundles of fur and bones are regurgitated by owls after a meal.

Other signs of animal life can be found on the pine needles. Little burrowed holes are clues that skunks or squirrels were looking for food, and piles of discarded pine cone scales at the roots of a tree are a sure sign that a squirrel has had a good meal. Also, when there is snow on the ground, look at the bases of tree trunks for minute snow fleas jumping by the thousands.

At the first junction go straight for a short distance, then take a right. (A left heads out toward Conant Road.) As the trail starts back up Pigeon Hill, take the first trail on the left. This passes through an opening in a stone wall and will take you back across the stream to Browning Field.

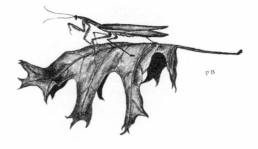

Beaver Pond/
Stony Brook South

General Information

These three parcels of conservation land, with the accompanying private land in between, comprise a diverse terrain of ponds, swamp, bog, and wooded upland, with an extensive network of trails, many of which are good cross-country skiing trails. Some of the land between Twin Pond and Beaver Pond is privately owned, with access available over trail easements. Please stay on marked trails at all times.

Parking

A private gravel driveway off Weston Road, 200 yards south of Woodcock Lane, leads to the Beaver Pond trailhead. A couple of cars may park on the right-hand side near Weston Road. Parking is also available by the riding ring at the north end of Browning Field North on Weston Road. From the south side, parking is available for a few cars at the gravel turn-off on the north side of South Great Road (Route 117) on the Weston/Lincoln town line. This portion of the Stony Brook South land is owned by the City of Cambridge and both parking and trail are intended to be ADA compliant in the near future. Limited parking is also available on Twin Pond Lane near the trail entrance.

Links to Other Trails

The Beaver Pond trails connect with Browning Fields to the north, with the Umbrello and Row Parcels to the west, and the Hunsaker conservation land to the east.

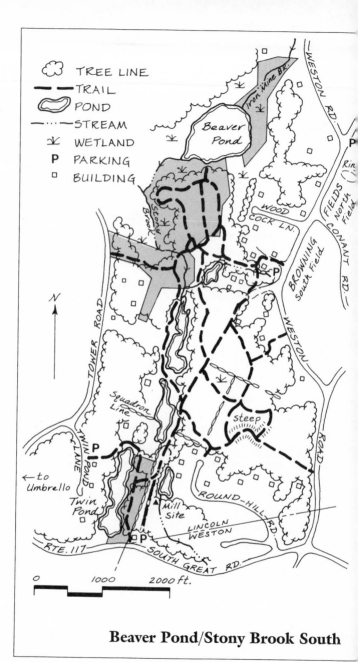

Beaver Pond/Stony Brook South

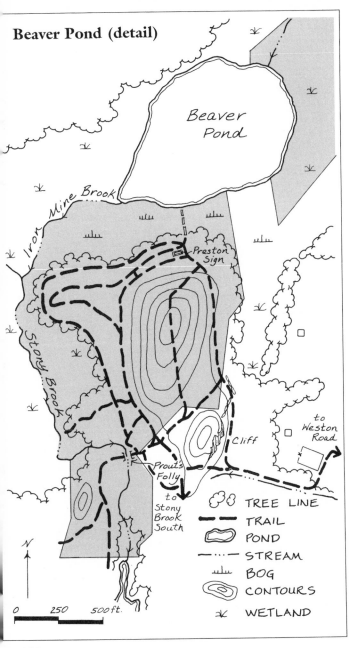

Beaver Pond (detail)

Beaver Pond

Iron Mine Brook

Stony Brook

Preston Sign

Cliff

to Weston Road

Prout's Folly

to Stony Brook South

N

0   250   500 ft.

⬯⬯ TREE LINE

– – – TRAIL

⬭ POND

----- STREAM

ᴜᴌᴜ BOG

◎ CONTOURS

⅄ WETLAND

121

History

In the early land grants in the 1600s, this land was divided
between Concord and Watertown, with the boundary between the two towns passing just east of Beaver Pond and
west of Twin Pond, roughly from north to south. At one
time, the Watertown side of Beaver Pond was part of an
old farm bought in 1702 by Captain Benjamin Garfield, an
ancestor of James A. Garfield, the twentieth President of
the United States. In Concord, the brook running into
Beaver Pond was the dividing line between the original
seventeenth-century Flint grant on the east and the Bulkeley Farm on the west.

Historically, the entire Beaver Pond/Twin Pond area
was used extensively for farming. The swamps were
dammed and ditched for hay, upland areas were used
for pasture and woodlots, and the brook was dammed for
sawmills and used as the location for a rope-walk, which
twisted fibers under water to make rope for the Revolutionary War effort.

Acquisition

Jean Wood Preston, wife of the longtime President of the
Lincoln Land Conservation Trust, Bill Preston, gave Beaver Pond and the surrounding land to the Lincoln Land
Conservation Trust. A memorial sign in the woodland
reads, "These woods in which for 30 years she so often
walked were given by Jean Wood Preston to the Lincoln
Land Conservation Trust so that others could enjoy her
perennial joy of nature." Twin Pond and the surrounding
land was a gift to the Lincoln Land Conservation Trust by
Constantine and Olga Pertzhoff. Through the generosity
of the Harrington and Hunsaker families and donations by
the Lincoln Land Conservation Trust, Rural Land Foundation, and private citizens, 54 acres of the Harrington land
and 36 acres of the Hunsaker land were permanently preserved since 2000. In addition to private generosity, the

Town of Lincoln also contributed to the Harrington project through the Community Preservation Act (CPA) and the City of Cambridge used Cambridge CPA funds as well as a state self-help grant to purchase a portion of the property for watershed protection; Stony Brook is in the Charles River watershed, which supplies water to Cambridge.

Natural History

Suggested Walk: Trail from Route 117 to Stony Brook and back

From the parking area on Route 117, look for a trail heading west towards Twin Pond. Near the beginning of this trail, a human-made outlet from the south end of Twin Pond may have once been associated with a saw mill. The drain, as it was called in a 1778 deed, continues eastward to Stony Brook. Further along this trail, a plot with a series of ridges in the ground was apparently once a tree plantation.

Continue on this trail to the north end of Twin Pond, where one can get a fine view down the length of the pond, which is largely covered with water lilies in the warm months. Nearby, a long ditch that once ran from the south side of Stony Brook swamp to Twin Pond is visible. On a summer afternoon one might hear bullfrogs croaking from the pond and a wood thrush or Eastern wood-pewee calling from the woods. Sweet pepperbush scents the air in late summer. A rattling call and flash of blue and white may alert you to the belted kingfisher, an active character that switches from perch to perch as it looks for small fish and dives headfirst to catch one.

Several ducks can be seen on the pond, including black ducks, mallards, wood ducks, hooded mergansers, and possibly buffleheads. Buffleheads, black and white water birds with white patches on their head, are most likely to appear during migration in March and April and October and November. A wood duck nest on the pond could alternatively accommodate hooded mergansers, which are known to favor the same kind of quiet water body that wood ducks prefer. Not only will the hooded mergansers eat the fish in the pond, but they will also take small frogs, crayfish, tadpoles, insects, and the roots and bulbs of water plants. Continuing on this trail leads to Twin Pond Lane and connections to the Umbrello trails.

From the north end of the pond, retrace your steps, and just before the trail climbs a steep knoll, take a left fork heading east into a small field. Cross the field and join the main trail (a gravel road) heading north. This trail runs parallel to a stone wall built before 1778 and crosses Stony Brook on a cement bridge. North lies a stone wall, running roughly east to west, that was the "Squadron Line against the fifth division," an historic boundary of Watertown's Great Divides. At one time this wall must have run from the Concord line, about 100 feet west of Twin Pond, through Waltham.

Deer, mink, and otters have been seen in these woods and swamps, and the ponds to your left attract a number of waterfowl species, including mallard pairs, which nest on little islets or in bushy clumps on the wetland shore. Tree swallows nest in the boxes provided, and Canada geese raise their goslings here annually.

Pectoral, solitary, least, and semipalmated sandpipers also make occasional appearances here. They wade in the mudflats created by the controlled water height, which is adjusted by removable boards at each dam site. In the shallows, the sandpipers probe for aquatic invertebrates while painted turtles bask on a log not far away. Dr. Harrington has for many decades managed this land to promote wildlife, especially birds.

Return south along the main trail, passing a pond on your left and the trail to Twin Pond on your right. The pond was the site of Harrington's grist and sawmill, in service from about 1783 to 1920.

Continue south along the woods road to Route 117 and the gravel parking area. Enroute, listen in spring and summer for the nasal ascending *wheeep* of the great crested flycatcher in the tree canopy.

Suggested Walk: Loop Trail to Beaver Pond from Weston Road

The trail begins to the left, at the end of the cul-de-sac gravel driveway off Weston Road, 200 yards south of Woodcock Lane. From the point where the trail turns right, it parallels a stream for a few hundred feet. This stream drains the swamp at Silver Hill and the wetlands east of Browning Fields. Further on, it joins Stony Brook. In April and May, look for marsh marigolds in sunny sections along this stream and for trout lilies, wild geraniums, and sessile bellwort flowers where there is dappled light not far from the trail.

Where the trail forks, starting the Beaver Pond loop, different stages of forest succession can be noted. This was pasture land as recently as 50 years ago, but when it was no longer grazed, gray birches, red cedar, and dwarf juniper were some of the first species to take hold. Now most of the sun-loving pioneers have been overtaken by rapidly growing white pines and red maples. Take the right fork.

To your left, one of several bedrock outcrops on the property is visible. The last glacier pushed over this ridge, forming a gentle slope on the far side and plucking pieces from the sheer face on this side. The outcrop is called a *roche moutonnee,* fleece rock in French, because it looks like a grazing sheep, in this case oriented north-south. Further down the trail, other rock outcrops have characteristic plants growing in the crevices—columbine, polypody fern, spinulose wood fern, and ebony spleenwort, an unusual little fern with alternate leaflets and a black stem.

Note the many stone walls, built by early settlers in the course of clearing the land to serve as cattle fences and property lines and now laced with boulder lichens. An observant person may notice shoots of American chestnuts, whose roots were not destroyed by the chestnut blight. The leaf is oblong, with prominent veins and marginal teeth. Only rare sprouts will grow beyond the sapling size; most will succumb to the blight before bearing fruit.

At Beaver Pond, a boardwalk leads out to the pond edge over a classic quaking bog. With a base of sphagnum moss, this quaking mat is the foundation for an interesting plant community in which heaths such as cranberry, swamp azalea, leatherleaf, and highbush blueberry are prominent, as well as a collection of other bog species, including tamaracks, pitcher plants, northern white violets, and sundews. Be careful not to step off the boardwalk; the bog plants are fragile and can easily be destroyed, and there is poison sumac along the pond's border.

Other interesting plant communities flank Beaver Pond. The most obvious zone around the pond is the emergent vegetative zone, dominated by water willow and sweet gale and dotted with maples, cattails, and tamaracks, which turn golden then drop their needles in fall.

Retrace your steps up the bank and bear right. As you progress down the trail, you may notice some Norway spruce scattered among the native white pines and maples. These, along with some balsam and hemlock, were planted as seedlings in 1952 by Bill Preston, who lived nearby (and to whom this guidebook is dedicated). The hemlocks, native to this area, are more tolerant of shade and have been more successful than the spruces, which appear as slightly stunted in growth, and the balsam, which have all but disappeared. In May, look for forest floor wildflowers that also love the shade, such as bloodroot, wood anemone, starflower and pink lady's slipper. Great-horned owls often nest in an abandoned hawk nest in a tall pine. While the female sits on the newly-hatched owlets in March, the male hunts the woods and lowlands for food, providing mice, squirrels, and even rabbits and skunks for his family. When the owlets are big enough, the female goes off to hunt too, and human neighbors can get a look at the tops of the youngsters' heads, their feathery ear tufts peaking up over the messy pile of sticks.

This loop continues back to the main trail. One of the

trail spurs to the right will lead a short distance to Stony Brook, which has been formed by the outlet from Beaver Pond and the brooks draining Flint's and Todd Ponds. This stream crossing is called Prouts Folly, perhaps for an unsuccessful scheme of an early colonist, Ebenezer Prout, who owned a nearby farm prior to 1702.

Retrace your steps to the main loop and out to Weston Road.

19
Umbrello/Fernald Woods

General Information

The Umbrello land is a pastoral 32-acre area with open fields, rocky ridges, and scrubby hedgerows. The open fields are used for produce farming and tree cultivation, and the abundance of seed-bearing field flowers and bushes and small trees for berries make it a good bird watching area in fall and winter. The Row property encompasses a lovely meadow, pine forest, and wetland. Its wetland system provides an important wildlife corridor leading from Umbrello north to the Donaldson/Andrysiak field. The Fernald Woods parcels include rolling hills, wetlands and uplands.

Parking

Parking for a couple of cars is available in a pull-off on Route 117 across from Old Sudbury Road, or on the east side of Twin Pond Lane by the trail marker.

Links to Other Trails

The Umbrello trails connect with the recently acquired Row and Fernald Woods properties, which lead to the Tower Road well site and the Beaver Pond Spur.

Acquisition

When the 45-acre Umbrello property was acquired by the Rural Land Foundation in 1979, several house lots were sold, making possible the preservation of the remaining land. The Row and Fernald Woods properties used this same model of limited development to preserve a meadow and pine forests, and to provide trail access and a wildlife corridor connecting Umbrello to the Tower Road well site.

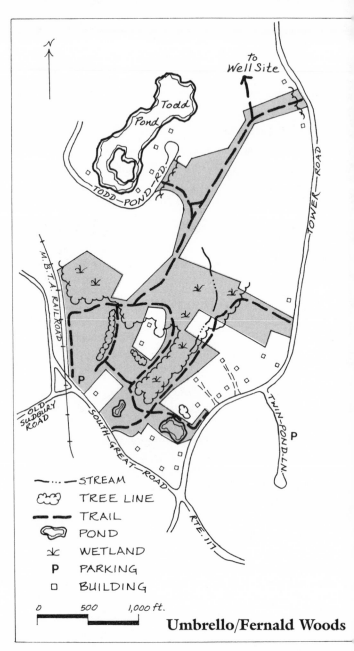

Umbrello/Fernald Woods

STREAM
TREE LINE
TRAIL
POND
WETLAND
PARKING
BUILDING

0   500   1,000 ft.

In addition, the Row project relied on the generosity of the Row family and neighbors, as well as the Town of Lincoln which participated through the Community Preservation Act. Neighborhood generosity was also important in the Fernald Woods acquisition.

Natural History

In summer, open sections of the Umbrello fields beyond the farmland are bright with black-eyed Susans, meadowsweet, tansy, evening primrose, mullein, and many other flowers. Other portions, where the vegetation has been filling in for years, are thick with honeysuckle, bittersweet, gray birch, burdock, small maples, young white pines, and multiflora rose.

The trees and shrubs provide good cover, so it is not surprising that there are a number of animal residents: woodchucks and foxes, which hide their burrow entrances under the brush, cottontail rabbits, and birds such as tufted titmice, sparrows, crows, blue jays, and wild turkeys. A walker might be lucky to flush a ring-necked pheasant. Since it was introduced from Asia, the pheasant has adapted well to North America, although the local population has been declining severely in recent years. On the Umbrello land, it finds the perfect combination of tall grass, low bushes, and briars for protective cover.

Suggested Walk from Tower Road

From Tower Road, the main trail leads over a small bridge and past a small pond to a large open field. This field is currently used by The American Chestnut Foundation as a research orchard, aimed at the reestablishment of a species which used to be the dominant forest tree in this area. Just before the field, a trail to the right circumnavigates the newly acquired Row Field, winding back to Tower Road about a hundred yards from the entry point. The chestnut seedlings growing in the field are hybrids of our native

American chestnut, which was largely wiped out early in the last century by the accidental introduction of a blight from Asia, and the Chinese chestnut, which can contribute blight resistance. In summer, all the native wildflowers and weeds are allowed to grow up between the tree rows so that deer, which love to nibble on the tender chestnut foliage, will have plenty of other browse to feed on. (Be careful not to stumble into an animal's burrow or den.)

The trail then ducks into lovely woods, passing a picturesque pond full of yellow pond lilies (*Nuphar variegatum*) in summer. This area also offers a rich jumble of goldenrod and wild grapevines as well as exotic, invasive species such as purple loosestrife and buckthorn.

After crossing a driveway, the trail skirts above the large Umbrello field used by Blue Heron Organic Farm to grow vegetables, herbs, and flowers. It then heads north into the Fernald Woods conservation land, a typical mature New England wood of white pines and oaks, with abundant American chestnut stump sprouts along the way. After passing a wetland and a small dam (over which a trail leads back to Tower Road), the trail rises to follow an esker up to the Lincoln well site, from which the trail goes back to Tower Road or down to Lincoln Road.

20
Stonehedge

General Information

Stonehedge is an isolated nine-acre parcel with a little pond and a short loop trail. The land is located southeast of Stonehedge Road. The first part of the trail crosses private property, to give access to the conservation land.

Parking

Parking for a couple of cars is available on the shoulder of the road by the trail entrance.

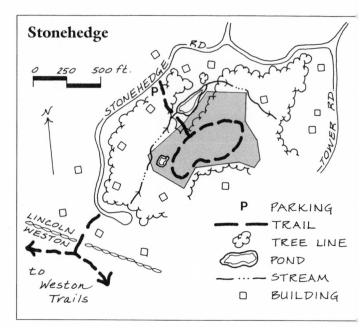

Stonehedge

P	PARKING
— —	TRAIL
🌳	TREE LINE
⬭	POND
—···—	STREAM
▢	BUILDING

Acquisition

The property was donated to the Lincoln Land Conservation Trust in 1964 by Bob Brownell as part of his initial development of the Stonehedge subdivision.

Natural History

This beautiful pocket of land is green with hemlocks, pines, yellow and white birches, mountain laurel, mossy rock outcrops, and an abundance of ferns, including royal, bracken, Christmas, and common polypody. A dense patch of the common polypody, meaning "many feet," blankets a hillock not far from the trail head. Thoreau described the mat-like colonies of this evergreen fern as "fresh and cheerful communities." Deer frequent the area; they like the cover of the coniferous woods and the freshwater wetlands on the property. The water also attracts many bird species, as do the berry-producing shrubs. Birds are likely to be seen in a large multiflora rose bush right next to the pond.

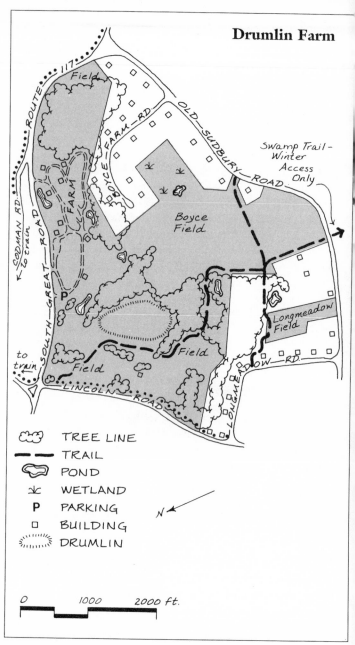

Drumlin Farm

Route 117

Codman Rd. — to train

South Great Road

Boyce Farm Rd.

Old Sudbury Road

Swamp Trail – Winter Access Only

Field

Boyce Field

Longmeadow Field

P

to train

Lincoln Road

Longmeadow Rd.

Field

Field

	TREE LINE
	TRAIL
	POND
	WETLAND
P	PARKING
□	BUILDING
	DRUMLIN

N

0   1000   2000 ft.

21
Drumlin Farm

General Information

Drumlin Farm Wildlife Sanctuary, a property of the Massachusetts Audubon Society, contains forests, ponds, cultivated fields, native wildlife displays and a farmyard, complete with pigs, sheep, chickens and cows. Teachers provide daily activities for visitors. Several miles of trails lead visitors through woodlands and pasture, past farm ponds and up to the sanctuary's namesake drumlin. The sanctuary is open 9 a.m. to 5 p.m. Tuesday through Sunday. In the winter (November through February), the sanctuary closes at 4 p.m. It is within walking distance of the Lincoln train station.

Picnicking is permitted only in designated areas. Vehicles of any kind (including mountain bikes), dogs, firearms, trapping, collecting, and alcoholic beverages are prohibited on the property. Skiing is also prohibited.

Lincoln residents and Mass Audubon members enter the sanctuary for free. Others must pay an entrance fee. A trail map is available at the admission window. Food grown at the farm following sustainable agriculture methods is for sale during the growing season, and the Audubon Shop offers a wide array of gifts, books and optics.

Parking

Parking is available in the lots at Drumlin Farm on Route 117.

History

The original 175 acres of Drumlin Farm were once eleven separate parcels, most of them in agriculture. Beginning in the seventeenth century, several related families settled and built farmsteads on what was then part of Concord. In 1735, one of the inhabitants, Josiah Parks, became an original signer of a petition to the Federal Court to set aside parts of Concord, including this portion, and sections of Lexington and Weston as a separate town, a goal accomplished in 1754 with the incorporation of Lincoln.

Between 1905 and 1920, Louise and Donald Gordon purchased eleven parcels to form one large estate and working farm. After Donald Gordon's death, Louise married Conrad Hathaway and continued farm operations, raising poultry and cattle and cultivating forage crops. The Gordons and later the Hathaways invited city children to experience farm life and learn how their food was grown. Since 1955, Drumlin Farm Wildlife Sanctuary has operated as an environmental education center that uses its farm and native wildlife displays to help people connect with the land and appreciate nature.

Acquisition

Upon her death in 1955, Louise Hathaway bequeathed the farm and land to the Massachusetts Audubon Society to be operated as a small bird and animal sanctuary. Just a year later, the Massachusetts Audubon Society established the Drumlin Farm Wildlife Sanctuary and moved its headquarters to the estate. Later the organization purchased two more parcels contiguous to the southern end of the property. In 1965 forty acres of farmland were purchased from the Boyce family and in 1993 twelve acres that were part of the Van Leer farm were added through cooperative efforts with the Rural Land Foundation and the Lincoln Land Conservation Trust. Farm activities have been diversified to include naturally grown vegetables and herbs and a full range of farm animals.

In 1954 the United States Government acquired the field at the site of the current overflow parking area and the top of the drumlin as part of a Nike missile site. Using good foresight, Mrs. Hathaway arranged for a long-term lease for the land that became used for administrative buildings and radar tracking at the top of the drumlin. The actual missiles and their silos were located nearby at a site on Oxbow Road in Wayland. In 1974 the government abandoned the site, and by 1984 Massachusetts Audubon had returned it to farmland.

Natural History

The most obvious geological feature of Drumlin Farm is the drumlin itself, a giant deposit of clay till formed during the last glacial retreat. This feature dominates the center of the property. It is a classic example of this particular landform with its whale-like shape, steep in the front in a northwesterly direction and tapering to a tail in the direction of the ice flow. On a clear day, from the top of the drumlin, there is a view of Mount Wachusett to the west and Mount Monadnock to the north. Surrounding the drumlin are other related features including old glacial sand deposits on the west side, a glacial eddy turned farm pond and, in some places, grooved rock surfaces. The drumlin helps form the divide between the Charles River and Sudbury River watersheds.

Though much of Drumlin Farm is still cultivated land and pasture, the variety of natural communities, inter-

mixed with the farm fields throughout the property, are rich in wildlife. Masked, smoky, and short-tailed shrews, seen only on rare occasions by humans, leave tunnels in snowy winter fields. Song birds of the cropland and the grassy and scrubby fields include field and song sparrows, indigo buntings, blue-winged warblers, killdeer, tree swallows and, more recently, bluebirds, the latter returning to carefully placed nest boxes. Atop the drumlin—mowed every one to three years to maintain the old field habitat— monarch, skipper, common sulphur, and swallowtail butterflies feed on nectar from flowers such as milkweed, ox-eye daisy, red clover, and Queen Anne's lace. On the south side of the drumlin, one of the fields is left uncut to attract breeding bobolinks. Coyote and red fox hunt for small mammals to feed their young in dens around the drumlin. Thickets border much of the agricultural land and provide hiding places for woodchucks, rabbits and deer, which all take advantage of the crops. In adjacent stone walls, short-tailed weasels and striped skunks make their homes. Thicket plants produce berries for the birds—dogwood fruits preferred by woodpeckers and cedar waxwings,

blackberries by catbirds and robins, and elderberries for wild turkeys and cardinals.

The six small ponds of the sanctuary are good places for wildlife watchers at any time of day or night. At dusk and nighttime, big and little brown bats skirt the water as they rely on high-pitched sonar to locate mosquitoes and other flying prey, and raccoons arrive to scavenge along the pond edges. In daylight, barn swallows dip low over the ponds, catching insects to bring back to nestlings in the rafters of farm buildings. Phoebes, too, often feed near damp areas between visits to their nests. In addition, black ducks, mallards, and Canada geese frequent the ponds, and appearances are made by green and great blue herons.

Many amphibians rely on these ponds for breeding: the spotted salamanders, shiny creatures dotted with yellow or blue; the American toad, often referred to as a hoptoad by New Englanders; and spring peepers, present in virtually every woodland pond in March or April.

Wooded areas cover portions of the Drumlin Farm sanctuary. There are oak stands, red pine plantations, old-growth pines and some planted spruces, firs and yews. On the forest floor, pink and white spots of color draw one's attention to Solomon's seal, lady's slippers, Canada mayflowers, and starflowers. The forested areas are stopovers each spring and fall for migratory birds. Birdwatchers have reported less common species such as the Kentucky warbler, yellow-throated vireo, and yellow-headed blackbird, and other regular transients including bay-breasted warblers. Pileated woodpeckers and barred owls are often seen and heard in the woods on both sides of Route 117.

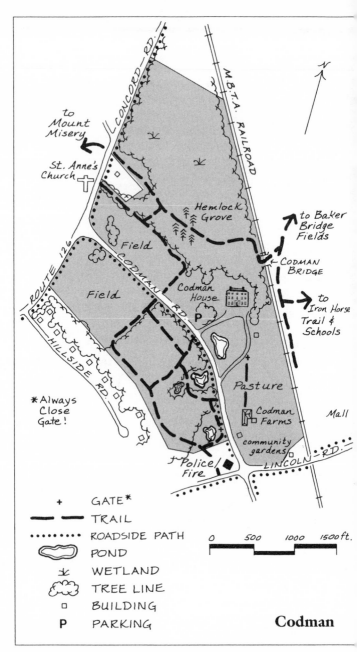

to
Mount
Misery

St. Anne's
Church

CONCORD RD.

M.B.T.A. RAILROAD

Hemlock
Grove

to Baker
Bridge
Fields

CODMAN
BRIDGE

ROUTE 126

CODMAN RD.

Field

Field

Codman
House

P

to Iron Horse
Trail &
Schools

HILLSIDE RD.

*Always
Close
Gate!

Pasture

Mall

Codman
Farms

community
gardens

LINCOLN RD.

Police/
Fire

+	GATE*
– – –	TRAIL
• • • • •	ROADSIDE PATH
POND
WETLAND
TREE LINE
□	BUILDING
P	PARKING

0   500   1000   1500 ft.

Codman

22
Codman

General Information

This area of town-owned conservation land, very accessible and appealing for both its human and natural history, includes more than 165 acres of hayfields, pastures, Codman House, Codman Farm, woods, and wetland.

Parking

Parking is available at the Lincoln Public Schools on Ballfield Road and just inside the main entrance to the Codman House. The school lot is the preferred area during cross-country ski season.

Links to Other Trails

Like a hub, trails from the Codman properties connect to Mt. Misery, the Baker Bridge Fields, Flint's Pond, the Bergen/Culver properties, and the Lincoln Public School land.

History

The Codman land is a portion of the 750-acre farm granted to Reverend Peter Bulkeley, a founder of the Town of Concord. For some time, it was referred to as the Goble Farm, although the Gobles were only tenants. In 1671, Timothy Prout bought it and maintained it with his son, Ebenezer, until 1700, when they began selling portions of the farm to different owners.

In 1708 Charles Chambers purchased the central and largest section, 275 acres, and subsequently added more land with the intention of forming a large country estate for his grandson, Chambers Russell, who would later be instrumental in the founding of Lincoln as a separate town.

By 1734 he had amassed an estate totaling 733 acres of land, along with six houses, seven barns, assorted outbuildings, and a weaver's shop. The family continued to farm the land, producing rye, hemp, flax, corn, oats, and English meadow hay.

Childless, Chambers Russell willed the estate in 1767 to his nephew, Dr. Charles Russell. When Dr. Russell, a Tory, fled his country property on the eve of the Revolutionary War, never to return, he forfeited his estate. However, his more patriotic father, James, was able to help his younger son, Chambers II, brother of Charles, acquire the estate. In 1790, the young Chambers Russell II died and willed the Lincoln farm to his nephew, Charles Russell Codman, then a six-year-old child.

Charles's father, John Codman, administered the estate for his son. A Boston merchant, John Codman envisioned a summer country retreat of European standards, and the farm reached its full potential during his management. He increased agricultural operations, converted the home to a three-story Federal-style mansion, erected new buildings, and planted exotic trees and shrubs. Illustrating the prominence of this farm, a nineteenth-century quote from the Gazetteer of Massachusetts reads, "Lincoln. . . .contains some of the best farms in the country. The most celebrated is that known at different times as the Russell, Codman, and Percival farm."

John's son, Charles, sold the estate out of the family in 1807, but ironically *his* son, Ogden, was able to repurchase it in 1861, and it remained in Codman ownership until 1968, upon the death of the last descendant, Dorothy Codman.

Acquisition

Dorothy Codman divided the estate in her will. She bequeathed the Codman mansion and the surrounding 16 acres to the Society for the Preservation of New England

Antiquities (now Historic New England), and another 25 acres of forest to the Lincoln Land Conservation Trust. The remainder of her estate was left in trust for the benefit of Lincoln; the Codman Trust has supported many endeavors in town.

The town of Lincoln acquired the remaining Codman land west of the railroad tracks. Since 1973, Codman Community Farms has operated a working farm with barns, a farm house, and 19 acres of agricultural land. Codman Community Farms is committed to preserving minor breeds of livestock; many of the sheep, cattle and pigs in the pastures and barns are hardy rare breeds. The organization also raises hay and silage corn on nearly 100 acres of land, mainly town conservation fields, thereby preserving the agricultural tradition in town. A large portion of the remaining acreage of the Codman estate was set aside as conservation land along both sides of Codman Road, now known as Codman North and Codman South properties.

An additional portion of the Codman estate was rezoned for Lincoln Woods, affordable housing, and commercial development (see next chapter for a more detailed explanation).

Natural History

Codman Community Farms uses the barns and surrounding 19 acres for pasture and community garden plots. In fall the community garden plots attract sparrows, which visit the abandoned, weedy gardens for seeds. The most common of them is the house sparrow, which is actually a type of weaver finch rather than a true sparrow. Since its introduction from Europe in the mid-nineteenth century, the house sparrow, which has several broods per year, has spread prolifically.

Possible sightings of similar-looking true North American sparrows include song, field, vesper, tree, white-throated and chipping sparrows. The white-throated spar-

row, a fall and winter visitor, has a beautiful song; even in fall it sings its sweet, nostalgic tune, *Old Sam Peabody, Peabody, Peabody*. The song sparrow, a spring and summer resident, sings repeatedly and in long phrases, for which it has been given the Latin name *melodia*. Thoreau described its sprightly song as *Maids! Maids! Hang up your teakettle-ettle-ettle*.

In the half light of summer mornings and evenings, twittering chimney swifts wheel and dart high above the open farmland, catching insects on the wing. Swifts do not perch on tree limbs or rest on the ground, but land only to feed their young or to sleep in chimney crannies, wells or hollow trees.

Canada geese are a familiar fall sight on Codman land, especially in the cornfield on Codman Road feeding on leftover corn kernels after the harvest. As the flock eats, sentinel geese keep watch for any threatening intruders; they are used to people, however, and are unlikely to fly because of human observers. An occasional pure-white snow goose or white-fronted goose, with an orange bill and a large patch of white on its breast, will join the flock for several days or weeks.

While walking the trails that border the fields on either side of Codman Road, you will pass weedy fringes of rough-fruited cinquefoil, yellow stargrass, and mullein. A trail on the north side of Codman Road wanders through woodland and a mature hemlock grove, probably planted by the Codmans. Wood for the beams and floors of the Codman Barn were harvested from this area. In a part of the mixed forest, an old dump lies nearly hidden. Periwinkle spreads nearby on the ground, an indication that once there was probably a dwelling close by. There is a big hemlock along the trail that has been split by lightning. Sadly, these hemlocks are being infested by the hemlock woolly adelgid, a tiny aphid-like insect which first appeared in Massachusetts in 1989 and has since spread to many parts of the state. It is a very expensive process to treat trees to withstand the damage done by these insects.

The overwhelming beauty of this area is the combination of large groves of hemlocks on both sides of the path with large groups of ferns. The hay-scented fern, which is light green in color, the cinnamon fern, whose fertile frond is a cinnamon color when ripe, and the interrupted fern are the most abundant. Halfway along this trail on the left is a large colony of New York fern. There are also smaller groupings of sensitive, lady and evergreen wood fern. Other plants along this trail include the Canada mayflower, lady's slipper, starflower and a variety of mushrooms.

On the south side of Codman Road, behind the police station, a trail encircles the wetlands, leading past two pools where wood frogs and spring peepers hold a chorus with birds when warm weather comes. Wild turkeys, barred owls, and pileated woodpeckers, as well as common yellowthroats, black-and-white warblers, redstarts, and ovenbirds breed in the vicinity. Among these strikingly colored and patterned warblers, the redstart is most vibrant. The male, black with small sections of contrasting orange-red, "pirouettes from limb to limb," notes ornithologist Frank Chapman, "like a village belle with coquettishly held skirts" as it pursues insects among the trees.

This section of the Codman property supports a wide variety of plants. The ground is covered with staghorn and shining clubmoss, and a variety of ferns. On the pond are fragrant water lilies, and around its shores are sedges that provide concealment for birds and other wildlife. Among the shrubs are swamp azalea and arrowwood viburnum. Red maple and white pine are abundant. Other plants that can be found here are pyrola (shinleaf) and leatherleaf, striped maple, and winterberry and American holly.

Between Codman Road and the wooded wetland is a sheep pasture. There on higher ground and bordered by a stone wall, red cedar and juniper flourish. At the pasture's edge, a chestnut oak, its bark deeply furrowed, branches widely to take full advantage of the sunny location. By the stone wall, burdock plants have grown to enormous size, producing hundreds of round clingy burrs.

23
Schools to Codman Bridge

General Information

Nearly 200 acres, this tract of conservation land in the center of Lincoln is made up of a patchwork of smaller parcels, extending from Baker Bridge and Sandy Pond Roads, past the Lincoln Public Schools to the Mall and railroad tracks, and to Woods End Road. Managed by the Conservation Commission and the Lincoln Land Conservation Trust as four properties, this land is a popular place to walk and ski, with easily accessible trails that pass through hayfields, woods, swamps, and a towering hemlock grove.

Due to extensive wetlands and sensitive slopes, mountain bikes are expressly prohibited on the trails in this area.

Parking

Parking is available at the Lincoln Public Schools on Ballfield Road.

Links to Other Trails

The trails connect with Flint's Pond and Pine Hill to the north and Codman and Mt. Misery to the west. The Gropius House, which belongs to Historic New England, is accessible by way of the trail to Woods End Road.

History

For several centuries this area was productive, working farmland that included pasture and meadow, hayfields and orchards, woodlots and tillage. Much of this land was originally part of the Bulkeley Farm (see Codman history). The Prouts sold to the Dakins the section that bordered on Flint's Pond. The Smith family, who later gave the land to the town for the schools, bought it from the Dakins in the

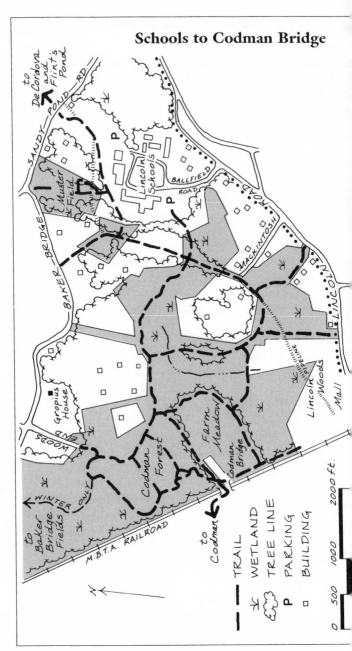

Schools to Codman Bridge

to DeCordova and Flint's Pond

SANDY POND RD.

P

Lincoln Schools

BALLFIELD ROAD

P

Muster Field

BAKER BRIDGE ROAD

MACKINTOSH

LINCOLN

Gropius House

Lincoln Woods

Mall

PIPELINE

WOODS END

Codman Forest

Farm Meadow

Codman Bridge

WINTER ONLY

Baker Bridge Fields

to Baker Bridge

to Codman

M.B.T.A. RAILROAD

TRAIL
WETLAND
TREE LINE
P PARKING
□ BUILDING

0   500   1000   2000 ft.

150

1700s. The Muster Field, in the northern section bordered by Sandy Pond and Baker Bridge Roads, is where the Minutemen of Lincoln gathered before marching to Concord on April 19, 1775.

Acquisition

Because the conservation land consists of many different parcels, acquisition of the property was complicated and took many years. One of the most creative approaches involved acquisition of Farm Meadow, in the southerly portion, which was part of Dorothy Codman's estate when she died in 1968. Farm Meadow is now hayed by Codman Community Farms, a community-run farm operation centered at Dorothy Codman's former barn complex. Her house was willed to the Society for the Preservation of New England Antiquities, (now Historic New England), 25 acres of forest were given to the Lincoln Land Conservation Trust, and the remainder of the estate was left in trust for the benefit of Lincoln.

The remaining 71 acres of Codman land, just east of the railroad tracks, was sold by the Codman Trustees to the Rural Land Foundation (RLF) in 1972. In a transaction that conserved much of the Codman East property, the RLF sold rights for a commercial development (now the Mall at Lincoln Center, reacquired by the RLF in 1997) recouping its investment and permitting the neighboring affordable housing called Lincoln Woods.

A study in 1967 had revealed that the reason for the departure of many residents was due to the increasingly high property and rental costs, which also discouraged town employees and people from outside Lincoln from settling here. One year after the study, 200 residents founded the Lincoln Foundation, a non-profit corporation, to build the town's first affordable multi-family community. Many town groups worked with the Lincoln Foundation, including the Planning Board, the Lincoln Land Conservation

Trust, the Rural Land Foundation and the League of Women Voters. In 1974, after six years of effort, total funding was secured from the Massachusetts Housing Finance Agency through a 40-year mortgage, and Lincoln Woods, with 125 units, became a reality. Wells Road was named for a beloved Town Clerk, George Wells, who warmly supported the project from the outset.

Natural History

Encompassing a wide area, the trails of this parcel wander through hayfields and swamps, over hills, past orchards, and through mature woods. Stone walls crisscross the land, evidence of past use as pasturage and cropland.

The Muster Field north of the Lincoln schools is completely open except for an uneven row of crab apples in the center. Wildflowers, however, such as goldenrod, Queen Anne's lace, and milkweed are abundant. The western side of the Muster Field is flanked by a scrubby wetland with lots of buttonbush, scarlet-stemmed red osier dogwood,

and portions with swamp maple and cattails, among which nest red-winged blackbirds, early arrivals in spring.

Broad-winged hawks may also be seen at the Muster Field in season, as evidenced by the local mimics, the blue jays, who have learned to copy the shrill broad-wing whistle *pee-teee*. Listen also for the high, faint trill of the American toad in the wet meadow on warm days and evenings in April and May as the males call in breeding season. At the northern end of the field behind Smith School are the remains of an old orchard through which goes a trail that leads to Baker Bridge Road. In the opposite direction, a trail follows the length of a long open field where the gas pipeline runs southward. Bittersweet, multiflora rose, and overgrown scrub growth on the field's edge attract berry-eating birds, including a territorial mockingbird that aggressively protects its prized berry clump from robins and other neighboring birds.

West of this field, the trail leads to wet woodland dominated by ash trees. It is a quiet place, undisturbed and secluded. The flat ground supports a few wetland plants such as royal fern and some highbush cranberry with ruby red fruits. On the side of the trail near Macintosh Lane, the ground is higher and drier and supports more year-round bird activity. Among the permanent residents are cardinals, brown creepers, and hairy woodpeckers. Possible summer locals include ovenbirds, wood thrushes, and orioles.

Suggested Walk: Loop trail beginning at the Lincoln Mall and circling through the woodland and returning to the Mall

The trail starts at the end of the commuter parking lot at the Lincoln Mall and proceeds along the dirt road that runs parallel to the railroad tracks. The railroad, which now carries commuters between Boston and Fitchburg, opened for service to Lincoln in June, 1844. At that time, the trains traveled between Charlestown and Concord, running four times daily in each direction.

After 250 yards, the dirt road enters a large field. Turn right and walk along the southeastern edge. This field, Farm Meadow, has been a part of working farms for many centuries. About midway down the field, there is a honey tree, occupied by honey bees. Listen for their buzzing and look for them flying back and forth to the tree with pollen from meadow flowers such as clover and daisy fleabane. Watch for coyotes, which are occasionally seen hunting along the field edge, close to their sanctuary in the forest.

Above the field, red-tailed hawks often circle as they look for voles and other prey. In spring and summer, nesters associated with the field edge include indigo buntings, yellow warblers, and catbirds. In the center of the field, the flags mark an area left unmowed until mid-July so that bobolinks that return yearly can breed in the grass. Raucous crows are also frequent visitors.

Continue along the edge of the field and turn right on a trail that goes through a large patch of shrubbery. The path here is bordered by sumac, which is common in disturbed areas and is easily identified by its red spikes of fruit, present even in winter.

The trail passes through a red maple swamp and into a pine, oak, and hickory woodland with hemlocks on hillsides and scattered clumps of white birch. Take care crossing several small streams over simple bridges. On entering the woods, notice the fallen logs in varying stages of decay on either side of the trail. These decaying logs are homes for many organisms, contributing to the creation of a rich soil layer that supports the trees, shrubs, understory herbs, and wildflowers of the forest. The most showy spring plants of these woods are bunchberry, pink lady's slipper, starflower, wild geranium, and escaped lily-of-the-valley. Abundant ground covers are princess pine, Canada mayflower, and partridgeberry.

In early spring, one is likely to see two common woodland butterflies. The mourning cloak is named for its appearance, which is reminiscent of a dark cape. Its dark purple iridescent wings edged with yellow make it easy to discover, especially when it flaps its wings, creating an audible click. Since it winters over as a mature butterfly, not a chrysalis, it may appear on any warm day early in the year. The tiny spring azure is also easy to find. It is a silvery violet-blue butterfly that first appears in late March and April. Though named for its initial presence in spring, this butterfly has multiple broods, so individuals may be found even into late summer.

Continue down the trail as it bears left into a small opening dotted with juniper and red cedar, which may be visited during fall migration by cedar waxwings and yellow-rumped warblers feeding on the evergreens' dusty-blue berries. Bear right briefly along the short end of this clearing and then turn left along the path. Continuing right here leads to Mackintosh Lane and Lincoln Road.

The trail continues into the woods at the westerly side of this opening. As you leave the clearing and enter the woods, notice clumps of low-growing evergreen club mosses on either side of the trail. After crossing another stream and continuing through the woods, turn left at the next trail intersection. A right turn here takes the walker toward the Lincoln Public Schools and on to the DeCordova Museum and Flint's Pond.

This trail leads in the direction of the Codman Bridge and follows an old farm road bordered by a stone wall running along the northern edge of Farm Meadow. This trail section was previously named "Three Sisters," for a clump of three trees—some say white birches, others say white pines—that once grew along the trail's edge. The sewage treatment facility for the nearby housing complex and shopping mall is located within a fenced area here at the edge of the meadow. Turn left before the Codman Bridge over the railroad tracks and return to the parking lot.

24
Tower Road Parcels

General Information

Peirce Hill, Donaldson/Andrysiak Field, Tower Road Loop, and Town Well, all accessible from Tower Road and fairly close to one another, are excellent sites for easy bird watching for those who would like to take a short stroll. The Peirce Hill trail circles a classic drumlin. Donaldson/Andrysiak Field is an open field with a mown path leading from Tower Road to Peirce Hill Road. The Tower Road Loop and Town Well site are directly across Tower Road from one another. A short loop trail leads through the woods and swamp of the Tower Road Loop.

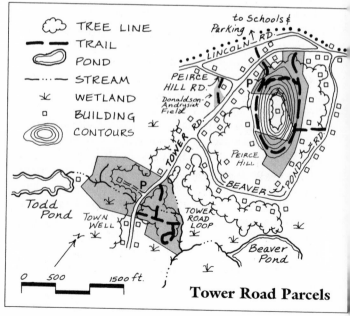

TREE LINE	
TRAIL	
POND	
STREAM	
WETLAND	
BUILDING	
CONTOURS	

to Schools & Parking

LINCOLN RD.

PEIRCE HILL RD.

Donaldson-Andrysiak Field

TOWER RD.

PEIRCE HILL

BEAVER

POND RD.

Todd Pond

TOWN WELL

TOWER ROAD LOOP

Beaver Pond

0   500   1500 ft.

Tower Road Parcels

Parking

Parking is available at the Lincoln Public Schools on Ball-field Road or on the shoulder of Tower Road for Peirce Hill and Donaldson/Andrysiak Field. Limited parking is available on the shoulder of Tower Road by the gate to the Town Well for Tower Road Loop and Town Well.

Acquisition

A portion of Peirce Hill was acquired by gift from the Stevenson family to the Lincoln Land Conservation Trust in 1975. In 1987 a group of neighbors was aided by the Rural Land Foundation in purchasing the remaining land.

The Tower Road Loop was a donation by the heirs of Pauline Todd, completed in 1976.

The Donaldson/Andrysiak Field was protected as part of the Lincoln Fields project with the transaction completed in 2004.

Natural History

Peirce Hill, also known as Horizon Hill, is covered by woods of pine, oak, hickory, ash, and hemlock. Buckthorn and a few witch hazel are also present on the rocky hillside, as well as some small escaped yews and American hollies. Growing on the forest floor is a carpet of ground cover—a Christmas fern colony on a north-facing slope, a huge blanket of periwinkle that has spread from plantings, and several patches of teaberry, spotted wintergreen, and pipsissewa.

Some particularly striking birds in brilliant colors have been observed on Peirce Hill. In summer, look for rose-breasted grosbeaks, scarlet tanagers and northern orioles in the forest canopy.

Suggested Walk: The Peirce Hill Trail.

The Peirce Hill Trail is an easy 20 minute stroll, of interest also to young children as it has much variety and it is short.

It can be accessed from the Lincoln Public Schools by walking out to Lincoln Road along the roadside path and crossing Lincoln Road from the middle of the island at the entrance to the schools.

It is difficult to see the trail from across the road, especially as there is generally traffic to dodge, but a trail goes up the hill along the south side of a stone wall and comes out on Tower Road. The Peirce Hill trail begins about 25 feet to the right (south) on the other side of Tower Road. The trail goes straight ahead for about 50 feet and then makes a right angle turn along the stone wall and heads south behind the red house at 24 Tower Road. After passing the red house, look for the junction where the trail rejoins itself after circling the hill. There is a swath of lily-of-the-valley immediately after the junction.

The trail continues south along the stone wall, passing through a large expanse of periwinkle. From here, the classic shape of a glacial drumlin can be seen, with a fairly steep southern side and a tapering slope to the north.

About halfway around the hill, a trail outlet drops down the hillside and emerges opposite #32 Beaver Pond Road. There is a well-placed trail post by a large oak tree. By going north on Beaver Pond Road for 50 feet and down the driveway of #28 and #30, it is possible to join the trail that winds over to the Pierce House. This outlet trail crosses a small seasonal rill, which can make it a bit wet in the spring, and there is considerable poison ivy at the beginning, but otherwise it is a great addition to the trail.

Continue on the Peirce Hill Trail another 5 minutes to a junction. The right fork leads directly to Tower Road at the foot of the long driveway up the hill. The left fork goes through an attractive pine and oak wooded area and slants down the hillside to rejoin the trail behind the red house.

The Donaldson/Andrysiak Field is filled with a diversity of grasses, sedges and wildflowers: milkweed, Joe-Pye weed, goldenrod, black-eyed Susan, spreading dogbane,

Queen Anne's lace, horse nettle, wild strawberry, little bluestem, and field bindweed. The field is lined by a narrow band of ash, Norway maple and sugar maple. The southwest corner of the property is forested and abuts a small wetland. White ash and elm are the dominant tree species in this area, and jewelweed and sensitive fern are common in the forest area and extend into the field. The field provides habitat for some ground nesting birds and mammals.

The Beaver Pond Spur and Town Well, with their lush wetlands, are ideal areas for finding warblers and other songbirds in spring and summer. From Tower Road, the trail to the Beaver Pond marsh follows along the top of an esker, a ridge of sand and sediment formed by water flowing through a tunnel under the glacier. As the path dips, it passes a giant three-trunked red oak on the left, then enters the swamp, where the chorus of bird song can be overwhelming in the spring.

The combination of the woodland and the beautiful sun-lit swamp, adorned with winterberry, cinnamon ferns, speckled alder and swamp azalea make this a perfect bird sanctuary. Both food and nesting sites are plentiful. In spring, migrant songbirds such as chestnut-sided, blue-winged, and yellow-rumped warblers pass through. The rusty blackbird, another transient which has been seen here, is a dark coal color with a yellow eye in spring; by fall, however, the feathers on its wings and head molt to become a rusty reddish brown.

In summer, scarlet tanagers, red-eyed vireos, swamp sparrows and several warblers have all been noted. For nesting, the black-throated green warbler chooses coniferous evergreens, most commonly white pine, and the yellow warbler likes shrubbery and low trees, especially alder by the swamp. Scarlet tanagers nest in the deciduous canopy, and red-eyed vireos prefer saplings. Whereas the male tanager's brilliant hue makes it easy to spot, the red-eyed vireo

is an inconspicuous green and is more likely to be heard than seen. The male's persistent and repetitive robin-like song is a commonly heard summer sound in the woods.

Insects are plentiful both above and below the water surface. Mosquitoes provide food for many birds on the wing, and the larvae are part of the underwater food chain. Watch for dragonflies speeding by or iridescent damselflies bobbing on a blade of grass in the sun. These insects, so often overlooked by humans, provide the food on which more popular animals, such as birds and frogs, survive.

Birds of Lincoln

2005 Edition

An informal list of birds seen in Lincoln
within the last twenty years.

Comments and additions for a future edition
of the list are welcomed by the
Lincoln Land Conservation Trust.

CODES AND DEFINITIONS

Seasons

Sp   Spring (March 1–May 31)
S   Summer (June 1–August 15)
F   Fall (August 16–November 30)
W   Winter (December 1–February 28)

Abundance

▬▬   Abundant and widespread; easily found and often in large numbers

▬▬   Common; easily found in the proper habitat

▬▬   Uncommon and/or local; generally seen only in small numbers or within very restricted habitats

– – – Rare but regular; recorded every year but usually hard to find

. . . . Very rare and irregular; not seen every year

✳   Irruptive species: erratically numerous in some years

Population Trend

↑   Increasing
↓   Decreasing

Habitat

A   Aerial
D   Near Dwellings
F   Forest
G   Grassland, field, meadow, pasture
H   Hedgerow, thicket, brushy field, forest edge
M   Freshwater marsh, bog, swamp
P   Pond, lake, stream, river
X   Anywhere

Name of Species	Sp	S	F	W	Habitat
Red-throated Loon	- - - -		. . . .		P
Common Loon	- - - -		———		P
↓ Pied-billed Grebe	- - - -		- - - -		P
Horned Grebe	. . . .				P
Red-necked Grebe			. . . .		P
↑ Double-crested Cormorant	———	———	———		P
Great Cormorant	. . . .		. . . .		P
↓ American Bittern	. . . .				M
↑ Great Blue Heron	———	▬▬▬	▬▬▬ - - - -		MP
Snowy Egret		. . . .			P
Green Heron	———	———	———		MP
Black-crowned Night-Heron	- - - ——— - - -				P
Turkey Vulture	———	———	——— - - -		A
Snow Goose	- - - -		- - - -		GP
↓ Canada Goose	▬▬▬	▬▬▬	▬▬▬	▬▬▬	GP
Mute Swan	———	———	———	———	P
Wood Duck	▬▬▬	———	▬▬▬		MP
Gadwall			. . . .		P
American Wigeon			. . . .		P
↓ American Black Duck	▬▬▬	———	▬▬▬	———	P
Mallard	▬▬▬	▬▬▬	▬▬▬	▬▬▬	MP
Blue-winged Teal			- - - -		P
Northern Pintail	- - - -		- - - -		P
Green-winged Teal	———		———		P
Ring-necked Duck	▬▬▬		▬▬▬ ———		P
Lesser Scaup			- - - -		P
Surf Scoter			- - - -		P
White-winged Scoter			. . . .		P
Bufflehead	- - - -		——— - - -		P
Common Goldeneye	- - - -		——— - - -		P

Name of Species	Sp	S	F	W	Habitat
Hooded Merganser	———	——	———	- - - -	P
Common Merganser	▬▬▬		▬▬▬	▬▬	P
Red-breasted Merganser			. . . .		P
Ruddy Duck	———		▬▬▬	▬▬▬	P
↑ **Osprey**	———		———		P
↑ **Bald Eagle**				- - - -	PA
Northern Harrier	- - - - - - - - - - ———				GM
↓ **Sharp-shinned Hawk**	———		▬▬▬	———	DFH
Cooper's Hawk	———	——	———	- - - -	DFHX
Northern Goshawk	- - - - - - - - - - - -			———	X
Red-shouldered Hawk	———	——	———	- - - -	HM
↓ **Broad-winged Hawk**	———	——	———		F
Red-tailed Hawk	▬▬▬	▬▬▬	▬▬▬	▬▬▬	AGH
Rough-legged Hawk				. . . .	G
↓ **American Kestrel**	——— - - - - - - - - - - - -				GH
Merlin	- - - -		- - - - - - - . .		GH
Peregrine Falcon	. . . .			. . . .	A
↓ **Ring-necked Pheasant**	. . . .				GHM
↓ **Ruffed Grouse**	- - - - - - - - - - - - - - - -				FG
Wild Turkey	———	——	———	——	DFGH
↓ **Northern Bobwhite**	. . . .		. . . .		GH
Virginia Rail	. . . .				M
Sora	. . . .				M

Abundance Codes: ↑ Increasing; ↓ Decreasing

▬▬ Abundant and widespread; easily found and often in large numbers.
—— Common; easily found in the proper habitat.
——— Uncommon and/or local; generally seen only in small numbers or within very restricted habitats.
- - Rare but regular; recorded every year but usually hard to find.
. . Very rare and irregular; not seen every year.
✱ Irruptive species; erratically numerous in some years.

Habitat Codes: A–Aerial; D–Near dwellings; F–Forest; G–Grassland, field, meadow, pasture; H–Hedgerow, thicket, brushy field, forest edge; M–Freshwater marsh, bog, swamp; P–Pond, lake, stream river; X–Anywhere.

Name of Species	Sp	S	F	W	Habitat
Killdeer	▬	▬	▬		DG
Greater Yellowlegs	· · · ·		· · · ·		MP
Lesser Yellowlegs			· · · ·		MP
Solitary Sandpiper	· · · ·		– – – –		M
Spotted Sandpiper	—	—	—		P
↓ Upland Sandpiper	—	—			G
Semipalmated Sandpiper			· · · ·		P
Least Sandpiper			· · · ·		P
Pectoral Sandpiper			· · · ·		GMP
Wilson's Snipe	· · · ·				GM
↓ American Woodcock	▬	—	—		GHM
↑ Ring-billed Gull	▬		▬	▬	P
↓ Herring Gull	▬	▬	▬	▬	AP
Lesser Black-backed Gull			· · · ·		P
Great Black-backed Gull	—	—	▬	▬	P
Rock Pigeon	▬	▬	▬	▬	DG
Mourning Dove	▬	▬	▬	▬	DFGH
Black-billed Cuckoo		—			FH
Yellow-billed Cuckoo	· · · · —	—			FH
Eastern Screech-Owl	—	—	—	—	FH
Great Horned Owl	—	—	—	—	FH
Barred Owl	– – – – – – – – – – – – – –	FM
Northern Saw-whet Owl	– – – –		—	· · · ·	F
Common Nighthawk	—	—	▬		AF
↓ Chimney Swift	▬	▬	▬		AD
Ruby-throated Hummingbird	—	—	—		DFH
Belted Kingfisher	▬	▬	▬	—	P
Red-bellied Woodpecker	▬	▬	▬	▬	DFM
Yellow-bellied Sapsucker	– – – –		– – – –		F
Downy Woodpecker	▬	▬	▬	▬	DFH
↓ Hairy Woodpecker	—	—	—	—	FH

Name of Species	Sp	S	F	W	Habitat
Northern Flicker	▬▬	──	──	- -	FGH
Pileated Woodpecker	──	──	──	──	F
Olive-sided Flycatcher	· · ·		· · ·		P
↓ Eastern Wood-Pewee	▬▬	▬▬	──		F
Willow Flycatcher		· · ·			H
↓ Least Flycatcher	· · ·				H
Eastern Phoebe	▬▬	▬▬	▬▬		DH
↓ Great Crested Flycatcher	▬▬	▬▬	▬▬		FH
Eastern Kingbird	▬▬	▬▬	▬▬		H
Northern Shrike				· · ·	GH
Yellow-throated Vireo	· · ·	· · ·	· · ·		HM
Blue-headed Vireo	──		──		FH
Warbling Vireo	▬▬	▬▬	──		H
Philadelphia Vireo			· · ·		FH
↓ Red-eyed Vireo	▬▬	▬▬	──		F
Blue Jay	████	████	████	████	X
American Crow	▬▬	▬▬	▬▬	▬▬	X
Fish Crow	· · ·	· · ·			A
Common Raven	· · ·	· · ·			A
Horned Lark				- -	G
Tree Swallow	▬▬	▬▬	──		GMP
N. Rough-winged Swallow	· · ·				P

Abundance Codes: ↑ Increasing; ↓ Decreasing

▇▇ Abundant and widespread; easily found and often in large numbers.
▬▬ Common; easily found in the proper habitat.
── Uncommon and/or local; generally seen only in small numbers or within very restricted habitats.
- - Rare but regular; recorded every year but usually hard to find.
· · Very rare and irregular; not seen every year.
✱ Irruptive species; erratically numerous in some years.

Habitat Codes: A–Aerial; D–Near dwellings; F–Forest; G–Grassland, field, meadow, pasture; H–Hedgerow, thicket, brushy field, forest edge; M–Freshwater marsh, bog, swamp; P–Pond, lake, stream river; X–Anywhere.

Name of Species	Sp	S	F	W	Habitat
Bank Swallow					P
Barn Swallow					DG
Black-capped Chickadee					DFH
Tufted Titmouse					DFH
Red-breasted Nuthatch*					DF
White-breasted Nuthatch					DF
Brown Creeper					F
Carolina Wren					DH
House Wren					DH
Winter Wren					F
Marsh Wren					M
Golden-crowned Kinglet					F
Ruby-crowned Kinglet					F
Blue-gray Gnatcatcher					FH
Eastern Bluebird					GH
Veery					FM
Gray-cheeked/Bicknell's Thrush					F
Swainson's Thrush					F
Hermit Thrush					F
↓ Wood Thrush					FH
American Robin					X
Gray Catbird					HM
↓ Northern Mockingbird					DH
↓ Brown Thrasher					H
European Starling					X
American Pipit					G
Cedar Waxwing					H
↓ Blue-winged Warbler					GH
Tennessee Warbler					F
Nashville Warbler					FH

Name of Species	Sp	S	F	W	Habitat
↓ Northern Parula	▬		▬		FH
Yellow Warbler	▬▬▬		- - -		MP
↓ Chestnut-sided Warbler	▬ - - - - - -				H
Magnolia Warbler	▬		▬		FH
↓ Black-throated Blue Warbler	▬		- - -		FHM
Yellow-rumped Warbler	▬▬		▬▬	· · · ·	FHM
↓ Black-throated Green Warbler	▬▬▬▬▬		▬▬		F
↓ Blackburnian Warbler	- - -		- - -		F
Pine Warbler	▬▬ ▬▬		- - · · · ·		F
↓ Prairie Warbler	· · · · · · · ·				FGH
Palm Warbler	▬▬		▬▬		GHM
↓ Bay-breasted Warbler	· · · · · ·				FH
↓ Blackpoll Warbler	▬▬		▬▬		FH
↓ Black-and-white Warbler	▬▬		▬▬	· · · ·	FH
↓ American Redstart	▬ · · · ▬				FH
Ovenbird	▬▬▬		- - -		F
Northern Waterthrush	- - -		- - -		MP
Common Yellowthroat	▬▬ ▬▬ ▬▬				HM
Hooded Warbler	· · · ·				H
Wilson's Warbler	· · · ·		· · · ·		H
↓ Canada Warbler	· · · ·		· · · ·		FH

Abundance Codes: ↑ Increasing; ↓ Decreasing

▬ Abundant and widespread; easily found and often in large numbers.
━ Common; easily found in the proper habitat.
── Uncommon and/or local; generally seen only in small numbers or within very restricted habitats.
- - Rare but regular; recorded every year but usually hard to find.
· · Very rare and irregular; not seen every year.
✳ Irruptive species; erratically numerous in some years.

Habitat Codes: A–Aerial; D–Near dwellings; F–Forest; G–Grassland, field, meadow, pasture; H–Hedgerow, thicket, brushy field, forest edge; M–Freshwater marsh, bog, swamp; P–Pond, lake, stream river; X–Anywhere.

Name of Species	Sp	S	F	W	Habitat
↓ Scarlet Tanager					F
↓ Eastern Towhee					FH
American Tree Sparrow					DGH
Chipping Sparrow					DGH
Field Sparrow					GH
Savannah Sparrow					G
Grasshopper Sparrow					G
Fox Sparrow					FH
Song Sparrow					DHM
Lincoln's Sparrow					H
Swamp Sparrow					HM
White-throated Sparrow					DH
White-crowned Sparrow					H
Dark-eyed Junco					DHF
Snow Bunting					G
Northern Cardinal					DH
Rose-breasted Grosbeak					FH
Indigo Bunting					GH
Dickcissel					DH
Bobolink					G
Red-winged Blackbird					GM
Eastern Meadowlark					G
Rusty Blackbird					M
Common Grackle					X
↑ Brown-headed Cowbird					X
Orchard Oriole					FH
Baltimore Oriole					DFH
Purple Finch					DF
House Finch					DH
Common Redpoll*					DH
Pine Siskin*					DF

Name of Species	Sp	S	F	W	Habitat
American Goldfinch	▬▬	▬▬	▬▬	▬▬	DH
Evening Grosbeak*	. . . .				DF
House Sparrow	▬▬	▬▬	▬▬	▬▬	X

UNUSUAL SIGHTINGS

Anhinga (April 18, 1991)
Cattle Egret (April 11, 1997)
Glossy Ibis (1997)
Greater White-fronted Goose (Oct. 20, 1991)
Black Scoter (October 28, 1995, 1999)
Mississippi Kite (June 2002)
Common Moorhen (Aug. 1991)
Hudsonian Godwit (Oct. 12, 2002)
Short-eared Owl (Nov. 2–15, 2000)
Whip-poor-will (April 30, 2001)
Yellow-bellied Flycatcher (May 28, 1994)
Alder Flycatcher (July 1996, May 30-June 7, 2005)
Western Kingbird (Oct. 1997)
Blue-headed Vireo (Dec. 29, 1991)
Sedge Wren (June 1993)
Bohemian Waxwing (May 1994, Feb. 1997)
Golden-winged Warbler (June 1994)
Brewster's Warbler (June 1997, Aug. 2001)
Lawrence's Warbler (July 1995)
Cape May Warbler (May 1996, May 22, 1998)
Black-throated Blue Warbler (Dec. 96)
Worm-eating Warbler (May 8, 2005)
Kentucky Warbler (May 1987)
Connecticut Warbler (Sept. 1997)
Mourning Warbler (May 2000)
Henslow's Sparrow (June 28-Sept. 11, 1994—nested)
Lapland Longspur (Nov. 24, 2000)
Yellow-headed Blackbird (1997)
White-winged Crossbill (Nov. 18, 2001)

Illustrations

All plants, (except the purple loosestrife) scenes, the cecropia moth co-coon, and the praying mantis, were drawn by Paul Brooks. The birds and mammals were drawn by Scott Hecker. The spotted salamander was drawn by Gwyn Loud and the purple loosestrife was drawn by Michael Musto.

Guidelines for Use of
Lincoln Conservation Land

These trails, fields, streams and forests represent generous gifts from earlier generations for all of us to enjoy. Please savor and respect these natural areas for active recreation and quiet reflection. You are in the same natural area that Henry David Thoreau explored more than a century ago. Help us to manage this open space appropriately for those who follow you, whether tomorrow or a century from now.

The following guidelines are an abbreviated summary of the detailed regulations that govern the access to and use of Lincoln conservation land. They are meant to provide a concise overview of regulation and safety considerations. Some detailed rules, associated with specific parcels, are discussed within the text devoted to that specific area.

I. General Information

Lincoln's conservation land is open for recreational use to individuals and small groups (less than ten), without permit, from dawn to dusk. Public trails are identified by signposts and by red, yellow, and orange discs. Many markers and posts have numbers and letters, which are part of a location system for public safety. In an emergency, please reference the nearest numbered marker. Lincoln Police and Fire can be reached in an emergency by calling 911.

The trails are specified for multiple use and, depending on the season, walkers, runners, horses, cyclists, skiers, and people on snowshoes may all be encountered. Please be respectful of others as you share this special place. Be careful not to harm domesticated animals or damage crops when passing cultivated fields. More detailed regulations are available from the Conservation Commission at the Lincoln Town Offices.

Motorized vehicles are not allowed on conservation land, including motorcycles, ATV's, and snowmobiles. Removal, damage, or import of any flora or fauna is not tolerated and hunting, trapping, or firearms are specifically prohibited. Smoking and fire building are also forbidden in order to help prevent the serious danger of a forest fire. In addition, consumption of alcoholic beverages is not allowed. All regulations are strictly enforced by Conservation Rangers and the Lincoln Police Department.

Visitors are reminded that portions of some marked trails are across private land whose owners' have generously permitted access. We are grateful to have these links and ask users to take special care in limiting noise, litter, and intrusions on personal privacy when using these passages. Keep strictly to marked trails. Enjoy your visit.

II. Parking

Please park only in the legally designated areas. Specific available parking is discussed within the text of each chapter devoted to individual conservation parcels. Parking is allowed only during daylight hours and roadside parking is prohibited in some areas. The blocking of gates and other emergency vehicle access points is forbidden and strictly enforced.

Parking is available in the municipal parking lot adjacent to the commuter rail platform, with a nominal fee charged during weekdays. Fees are not currently collected on weekends. No recreational parking is allowed in the main lot of the Mall at Lincoln Station. Parking for cross country skiing is designated at the Lincoln Schools, off Lincoln Road, where there is good access to conservation trails.

III. Dogs, Horses, and Bicycles

In general, pets are welcome to accompany owners on Lincoln conservation trails. There are a few exceptions in high traffic areas such as Mount Misery, where special posted restrictions apply. Particular restrictions are discussed within the individual chapters; signs exist in many locations, at trail heads and parking lots. All dogs are required to be licensed and vaccinated, and must be kept in sight and under voice control at all times. Owners are required to carry a leash and are asked to remove dog feces from trails. It is imperative that dogs be on leash when crossing a field which might contain domesticated animals or crops.

Horses may be ridden in the Browning Field ring and the open fields of Tanner's Brook area. Cross country riding is limited to trails only. There are a few wetlands and otherwise sensitive areas where riding is prohibited; these are clearly marked. Riders must keep their mount under control at all times and horses are not allowed to gallop on woodland trails. Please avoid seasonally wet areas where mud holes and other hazards may be encountered or created.

Bicycle riding is restricted to trails that have bike markers. All trails are generally closed to bicycles from January 1st through April 30th when the weather is unusually wet and trails are most susceptible to damage. Bike riders should maintain control and be able to dismount at all times. Walkers, horseback riders, and runners have the right of way.

IV. Additional Important Information

Flint's Pond is the main drinking water supply for the Town of Lincoln. No activities are permitted on or in the pond, or on the immediate adjacent shoreline. Please stay on the marked trails.

Use of conservation land is at your own risk; the Town of Lincoln, The Lincoln Land Conservation Trust, and private landowners assume no liability for injuries to persons or damage to property while on conservation land. Groups larger than ten require a permit.

Please enjoy your visit. If you have any questions or comments, please contact the Conservation Commission at the Town Offices (gumbartt@lincolntown.org or 781–259–2612) or the Lincoln Land Conservation Trust (llct@lincolnconservation .org or 781–259–0199). In case of an emergency dial 911.